FRANCESCA MARTINEZ

Francesca* is a comedian, write
toured the globe with her award
launched her comedy career in
and only woman to win the Open ᴍᴵᴄ
Fringe. She has performed in Australia, Ireland, France, Sweden,
Switzerland, South Africa, Canada, Singapore, Malaysia, and
America.

From 2003 to 2008, Francesca toured her hit Edinburgh solo
shows *I'mperfect* and *In Deep* around the UK. From 2011
onwards, she toured her award-winning show *What The *** Is
Normal?!* around the world, clocking up 140 dates and winning
the Edinburgh Fringe Media Network Award 2011. In 2016, she
supported Frankie Boyle on his sell-out UK tour, and was
commissioned to write a new comedy show, *Francesca
Martinez's Wobbly Manifesto*, for performance at museums
around the UK.

Since starring in five series of BBC1's *Grange Hill* in the 1990s,
Francesca has made numerous TV appearances including BBC2's
Extras opposite Kate Winslet and Ricky Gervais, headlining *The
Jonathan Ross Show* and guesting on *The Frank Skinner Show*.
She has also appeared on CBBC's *The Dumping Ground* and Sky
One's *The Russell Howard Hour*, as well as opening Series 11 of
BBC2's *Live at the Apollo*.

Francesca made global headlines in 2008, when she became the
first Olympic Torch-Bearer to pull out of the London relay in
protest at China's treatment of Tibet. In 2012, she made a splash
when she took on Michael Portillo live on BBC1's *This Week*.
She has since guested on Channel 4 News, BBC2's *Newsnight*,
BBC1's *Today's Politics*, and was voted most popular guest on
BBC3's *Free Speech*. Her 2019 debut on BBC1's *Question
Time* was described as the show's 'best-ever moment' and went
viral, with eleven million views in the first week alone.

Francesca's radio credits include several hugely popular
appearances on BBC Radio 4's *The News Quiz* alongside the
late, great Jeremy Hardy, and writing and performing for *The

* Francesca has cerebral palsy but much prefers the word 'wobbly'.

Verb and *Shakespeare's Centenary* on BBC Radio 3. In 2018, she wrote and starred in her first radio play *How We're Loved* for BBC Radio 4.

Francesca's best-selling book, also called *What The **** Is Normal?!*, was published by Penguin Random House in 2014. It garnered rave reviews and was nominated Best Book in the Chortle Comedy Awards and runner-up in the Bread & Roses Book Award. In 2021, she contributed to the anthology *This Is How We Come Back Stronger* for & Other Stories and the Feminist Press and, for TV, wrote the CBBC comedy-drama *How I Found My Two Best Friends*, which aired that same year.

A regular commentator on TV and radio, Francesca delivers motivational and after-dinner speeches across the globe. In 2005, she was nominated for the Motivator of the Year Award along with Sir Bob Geldof. She was awarded Public Affairs Achiever of the Year 2013, nominated a Top Ten Game Changer in BBC Radio 4's Woman's Hour Power List 2014, and Hero of the Year in the European Diversity Awards.

Francesca has recorded a popular TEDx talk, collected 100,000 signatures for the WOW campaign, which led to a historic debate in the House of Commons, and received a standing ovation from the Cambridge Union. She has an Honorary Doctorate from the Open University 'for making Britain a more compassionate and fairer society', and a second honorary doctorate from Bradford University 'for her contributions to equality, inclusive thought and social commentary'.

All of Us is her first stage play.

Francesca Martinez

ALL OF US

NICK HERN BOOKS

London

www.nickhernbooks.co.uk

A Nick Hern Book

All of Us first published as a paperback original in Great Britain in 2022 by Nick Hern Books Limited, The Glasshouse, 49a Goldhawk Road, London W12 8QP

All of Us copyright © 2022 Francesca Martinez

Francesca Martinez has asserted her right to be identified as the author of this work

Cover image of Francesca Mills, Francesca Martinez and Bryan Dick; photograph by Laura Pannack

Designed and typeset by Nick Hern Books, London
Printed in Great Britain by Mimeo Ltd, Huntingdon, Cambridgeshire PE29 6XX

A CIP catalogue record for this book is available from the British Library

ISBN   978 1 84842 924 6

Woodland
CARBON
www.woodlandcarbon.co.uk
NICK HERN BOOKS
Printed on Carbon Captured paper

All of Us was first performed in the Dorfman auditorium of the National Theatre, London, on 4 August 2022 (previews from 27 July). The cast, in order of speaking, was as follows:

RITA/DR ANDERSON/ANGELA	Lucy Briers
JESS	Francesca Martinez
NADIA/MARCELLA	Wanda Opalinska
LOTTIE	Crystal Condie
YVONNE/ANITA	Goldy Notay
AIDAN	Bryan Dick
POPPY	Francesca Mills
DOM/BOB	Oliver Alvin-Wilson
HENRY	Kevin Hely
HARGREAVES	Michael Gould
RAYMOND/POLICE OFFICER	Daniel Fearn
RYAN/OFFICER CHALFONT	Chris Anderson
KYLE	Christopher John-Slater
ENSEMBLE	Bonnie Baddoo
	Mat Betteridge
	Peter Eastland
	Rebecca Todd

Other parts played by members of the company

Director	Ian Rickson
Set and Costume Designer	Georgia Lowe
Lighting Designer	Anna Watson
Movement Director	Lucy Cullingford
Composer	Stephen Warbeck
Sound Designer	Gregory Clarke
Fight Director	Terry King
Company Voice Work	Jeannette Nelson
Staff Director	Hana Pascal Keegan
Project Producer	Christine Gettins
Production Managers	Tabitha Piggott
	and Anthony Newton
Casting	Isabella Odoffin CDG
Additional Casting	Alastair Coomer CDG
Stage Manager	Mica Taylor
Deputy Stage Manager	Emma Tooze
Assistant Stage Manager	Ian Connop

Acknowledgements

Firstly, I must thank the wonderful Rufus Norris for commissioning my first play. His belief in this project has been unwavering, especially throughout the challenges of Covid and lockdown, and I can't put into words how much I appreciate his support. I'm also deeply grateful to have had the amazing Emily McLaughlin as Dramaturg. Her advice and encouragement were invaluable in helping me develop each draft.

Heartfelt thanks to my brilliant father, Alex, who generously shared his extensive writing experience with me on every draft and taught me so much about playwriting. Thanks also to my incredible mum, Christina, and to my gorgeous brother and best friend, Raoul, for their insightful notes and sterling support. I must also mention my beloved grandfather, Yayo, who helped me find my passion for writing, and my grandmother, Yaya, who showered me with love and apple pie. I miss them every day.

I'm also massively grateful to Rick Burgess for casting his expert eye over the play and helping make sure the details were as accurate as possible.

As always, I have to thank my soul-mate, Kevin, for igniting my love of theatre, being my partner in crime, and helping me to be brave when I need to be. There's nobody I'd rather share this adventure with.

I feel so lucky to have had such a talented cast and crew on this production, and I thank each and every one of them for being so awesome to work with. Being closed down by Covid in March 2020, the night before out first show, has only turbo-charged our desire to share this play with the world.

Lastly, I must express a million thanks to my director, Ian Rickson, who, from the moment I met him, expressed such a deep passion for this play that I thought I must be dreaming. His sensitivity, wisdom and genius have made every moment we've worked together a complete joy. He is the best director I could have hoped for and, above all, a beautiful human being.

F.M.

To all those facing these battles for real.
May your words be heard.

And to the people who inspire me daily to fight
for a kinder world, especially:

Kevin

Mum and Dad

Raoul

Yayo and Yaya

Aaron

Yanis and Danae

Eden

Dr Bob

Mya, Clara, Maya and Gaia

Rick

Jeremy and Katie

Nicoleta and Rumi

Jeremy and Laura

Sedra

Characters

JESS, *late thirties, has cerebral palsy*
RITA, *early fifties*
NADIA, *Polish, a carer*
LOTTIE, *early thirties, mixed race*
YVONNE, *a disability assessor*
AIDAN, *late thirties, one of Jess's patients*
POPPY, *early twenties, wheelchair user, of restricted growth,
    Northern*
DOM, *young man, black*
DR ANDERSON, *female doctor, Scottish*
ANITA, *Oliver Hargreaves's assistant*
HENRY, *late forties, ex-soldier, Irish*
HARGREAVES, *sixties, politician*
RAYMOND, *middle-aged*
RYAN, *young man*
KYLE, *young man with cerebral palsy, wheelchair user*
BOB, *forties, black*
MARCELLA, *forties, Bob's wife, wheelchair user*
ANGELA, *fifties, a carer*
OFFICER CHALFONT

And FEMALE ADVISER, SOUND WOMAN, COMMUNITY
MEETING ATTENDEES, POLICE OFFICERS,
CAMERAPERSON

Note on Text

A dash at the end of a line indicates the next line cuts in.

*A forward slash (/) within a line indicates when the next line is
spoken.*

*This text went to press before the end of rehearsals and so may
differ slightly from the play as performed.*

ACT ONE

Scene One

A therapy room. Two armchairs.

JESS *walks in. She is in her late thirties and has cerebral palsy, which affects her coordination, speech and mobility. She holds the arm of her carer,* NADIA, *a Polish woman. They walk over to a chair and* JESS *sits down.* NADIA *hands* JESS *a water bottle, then leaves.* JESS *sips some water and waits.*

RITA *enters. She is in her early fifties. She is wearing a face mask and carrying a handbag.*

RITA. Sorry I'm late, Jess! Erm, it took a while to...

She takes off her coat and mask, and sits down in the empty chair.

Okay. Let's start... Actually, do you mind if I clean my hands? Just touched my mask!

JESS *shakes her head.* RITA *rummages through her bag and takes out some hand sanitiser. She cleans her hands thoroughly, then puts the sanitiser away.*

Ah, what a morning!... Hope you weren't waiting ages for me?

JESS. No, don't worry.

RITA shakes her hands dry. She gets a notepad and pen out of her bag and opens up the pad.

RITA. That's better. We can start now. Hello, properly, Jess.

JESS. Hello, Rita.

RITA. How are you?

JESS. Good, thanks. How are you?

RITA. I'm okay…

JESS. So… I wanted to follow up on our last session.

RITA. Right…

JESS. We talked a lot about how hard it was to leave the house.

They sit in silence for a moment.

RITA. On that note… Ooh… It hasn't been a great week.

JESS. Why not?

RITA. I only made it out once.

JESS. Where did you go?

RITA. I ran out of tobacco. Took me thirty minutes to leave the house… I really thought… I thought I was getting better. I *was* getting better. Can I clean my hands again? There's a bit of dirt here. (*Holds one of her hands up and points to a spot.*)

JESS. Let's just talk a bit more. How was your journey here?

RITA. It took me a long time to leave. As I said. Then, oh, the bus was crammed. Felt like a sardine! Bus, rush hour, what did I expect? Some people got a bit close for my liking. But I managed not to touch anyone, I think. Wanted to get a cab but… tad broke!

JESS. How long did it take you to leave the house?

RITA. Er, an hour and a quarter. Thereabouts. I checked the oven was off thirty-two times. God!

JESS. Did you try doing what we talked about?

RITA. Yes. But… Sorry, Jess. I thought I'd turned a corner! (*Sighs.*) Confession – I nearly cancelled today! My thumb was hovering over your number. But I didn't want to let you down, so…

JESS. I'm glad you made it. Well done.

RITA. I'm being congratulated for leaving my house! What a fuck-up… Sorry!

JESS. Why do you think things have felt more challenging lately?

RITA. Things always get tricky this time of year... I hoped they wouldn't this year. Because of you. Coming here twice a week... There's fourteen lamp posts on this road and seven trees, in case you didn't know. You're welcome. Can I clean my hands again?

JESS. Can you tell me why things get tricky around now?

RITA. It first happened this month. (*Laughs nervously.*) The eleventh, to be exact... The clock downstairs chimed eleven. I remember staring at the ceiling, counting the chimes. They went on and on. One, two, three, four, five, six, seven, eight, nine, ten, eleven. I kept counting. Over and over. Until he stopped. I did that every time it happened.

> *Beat.*

> I've never told anyone that. Those details. Eleven o'clock on the eleventh. I don't like the number eleven. Surprisingly!

> RITA *gets out the hand sanitiser and cleans her hands again.*

> At least, since Covid, people think I'm less weird doing this!

> *She shakes her hands dry.*

> Do you feel sorry for me? I'd hate that! (*Flinches.*) Really.

JESS. I feel sorry that you had to go through that. But you're here facing it. That's strong.

RITA. It's also his birthday this month. The eighteenth. That's always... Hmmmm...

JESS. Go on...

RITA. Confused. It's a confusing day because I feel love for him... He was like a father to me in some ways. Is that sick?

JESS. No.

RITA. That's a relief. I always thought if I said it out loud, you'd think I was nuts!

JESS. No. I don't think that. It's something I've heard before, actually.

RITA. Really?... Sometimes I'm crying and then I start laughing. I don't know... I want it to be not all heavy and doom and gloom. I'm fifty-one, for God's sake. I want to move on from it. I want to be able to leave my house like everyone else without thinking about it. I want to be able to touch people and be touched. I want to be free... I used to be like you, Jess, you know.

JESS. How do you mean?

RITA. Light. I had light in me.

Scene Two

JESS*'s living room/kitchen. Compact and simply furnished but homely. A sofa, small kitchen table and two chairs. An exercise bike in the corner.*

JESS *sits at the table with a bowl and a mug with a straw in it in front of her. She wears jeans, boots and a pyjama top with buttons. She's trying to undo the buttons.*

NADIA *rushes in, carrying some shopping bags. She speaks with a Polish accent.*

NADIA. Just dropping you off some milk!

JESS. Oh, Nadia!

NADIA. I thought Lottie might forget... (*Indicating bags.*) I'm taking these to Poppy. She was out of food again yesterday so...

She puts down the bags, takes out the milk and puts it on the table.

JESS. Actually, now you're here, can you...? (*Points to her buttons.*)

NADIA. Sure. Wasn't Lottie helping you today?

JESS. She didn't come home last night…

NADIA. Useless girl. Always letting you down! Okay. (*Walks to* JESS *and undoes her buttons*.) You should meet Poppy…

JESS. Does she live at number eighty?

NADIA. Yeah. I keep telling you this. I think you'd get on!

JESS. Why?… Cos we're 'DISABLED'?!

    NADIA *looks awkward*.

    I'm joking!

NADIA (*laughs and shakes her head*). Matko Boska! She'd love to meet you! She was so lonely in lockdown. Honestly, she…

    Her mobile rings. NADIA *answers*.

    I was just talking… What?… Are you okay?… I'm coming! (*Hangs up the phone*.) Poppy have asthma attack. Last night, the carer didn't leave inhaler by her bed!

JESS. Course. Go!

NADIA. You haven't eaten, have you? Have this.

    She takes a box of cereal out of a shopping bag and puts it on the table.

    And you have your assessment thing today. Good luck!

    She dashes to pick up the shopping bags.

    And make sure you call that Lottie. Okay? Bye!

    NADIA *leaves.* JESS *tries to open the cereal box. It's hard but she succeeds. She tries to pour the cereal into the bowl, inadvertently shaking cereal on to the table and floor.*

JESS. Ah, shit!

    She gives up and sips a bit of water from the mug. She tries to sweep up the cereal but it is too difficult. She shuffles over to the sofa, takes off her pyjama top and sits in her bra.

The front door opens. It's LOTTIE. *She is in her early thirties, mixed race and full of restless energy. She is all dressed up and looks like she has been up all night. She is on the phone.*

LOTTIE (*on phone*). I've got to go, Mum.

She ends the call.

JESS. Oh, made it home at last?

LOTTIE. Nice welcome!

LOTTIE *peels off her coat and dumps it on the floor.*

Ow, these shoes are torture! You are so lucky you can't do high heels. (*Kicks off shoes and stretches out her feet.*) Ah, what a relief! Mum's just been on at me to visit her. She's ill. I'm selfish. Full-on guilt-trip! I'll have to go and see her. Yippee. (*Rubs her feet.*) Knackered.

JESS. Sam?

LOTTIE. Don't give me that judgy face! (*Rubs her temples.*) God, I need sleep!

LOTTIE *flops down on the sofa, lies back, and shuts her eyes. She sits up suddenly.*

Wait, is it your POP thingy today?

JESS. PIP.

LOTTIE. So why are you half-dressed?!

JESS. Because someone said they'd help me this morning.

LOTTIE. Balls! Sorry. I forgot! (*Jumps up.*) Head's all over the place. I'm on it. Hey, why didn't you call me as soon as you got up? Stupid question! (*Walks to the table and sees the mess.*) Is this your plan? (*Laughs.*) Get the assessor to walk into a bomb site… to show how crap you are at preparing food? When are they coming?

JESS. Half-ten.

LOTTIE (*checking her watch*). Oh, my God!

She rushes into the bedroom.

What do you need? Sorry again!

JESS. A top.

LOTTIE returns with a top and helps JESS into it.

LOTTIE. This really is crazy. You being reassessed. I mean, it's not like you're going to be…

JESS. De-wobblied?

LOTTIE. What a total waste of time! Are they really going to keep reassessing you?

JESS. Yep.

LOTTIE. Someone's going to keep coming round here to ask you…

JESS. 'Are you still wobbly?' Yep. I should just say, 'How about I give you a wet shave and we'll find out?'

LOTTIE laughs.

LOTTIE. I could be here. When she comes? I called in sick.

JESS. When are you going to quit?

LOTTIE. Oh, Dad will love that… (*Imitates her dad.*) 'Unemployed at thirty-three'!

JESS. Have you told him yet?

LOTTIE. Shall I stay? And give her the evil eye.

JESS. I'll be fine.

LOTTIE. Let me stay. For moral support? I'd want someone.

JESS. I'm not you! Sorry. It's not a big deal, okay? I'm wobbly. They have eyes. That should be enough.

LOTTIE. I'll clear up.

She sweeps up the cereal on the floor with a brush and pan, but leaves the mess on the table.

Next time I forget I'm meant to be here – and there will be a next time – just call me, okay? Never feel bad about asking for help… Trust me, I'm the world's bloody expert at it! (*Spots the milk.*) I was meant to buy milk, wasn't I?

JESS. Nadia popped it round.

LOTTIE. Good old Nads. I love how little faith she has in me! Have you eaten?

JESS. Not hungry.

LOTTIE. I know how much you hate talking about what you can't do.

Beat.

JESS. Don't look at me like that. I'm not going to pour my heart out to you.

LOTTIE. Ha, you never pour your heart out to me!

JESS. That's cos I'm crap at pouring, innit?

LOTTIE *puts on her coat and shoes.* JESS *shuffles to the table and sits down.*

LOTTIE. If I don't see you later, I'll call from Mum's. And moan. Apologies in advance. You okay?

JESS. Stop worrying!

LOTTIE *hugs* JESS.

LOTTIE. Good luck, hun! Give her a wet shave, ha!

LOTTIE *opens the front door, nearly bumping into* YVONNE, *the disability assessor. She is very formal and appears slightly nervous.*

YVONNE. Er, hello, Jessica Flores?

LOTTIE. No, I'm her flatmate.

She points to JESS. LOTTIE *leaves.*

JESS. Hi. Come in.

YVONNE. Thank you. Sorry I'm late.

YVONNE walks in. JESS goes to shake hands but YVONNE elbow-bumps her instead.

I'm Yvonne Gupta. I'm from the Independent Assessment Services. I'm here for the Personal Independence Payment Assessment.

She shows JESS a lanyard hanging around her neck. It's the wrong way round.

Oops! (*Turns the lanyard round.*) There.

JESS. Please sit down.

YVONNE. Yes, sure. Right... I'll just take off my... Get myself sorted.

She clocks the messy table. JESS looks embarrassed.

JESS. Sorry about the mess. Feel free to move anything...

YVONNE sits opposite JESS at the table then opens her bag and takes out a chunky laptop.

YVONNE. Latest model. Not! Okay... Do you have two forms of identification at hand?

JESS. Yes.

She reaches for the items on the table, accidentally knocking off a book. YVONNE picks it up.

Oops. Thanks.

YVONNE checks the documents.

YVONNE. Thank you. (*Hands them back but they fall on the floor.*) Now I'm dropping things! It's infectious!... Sorry! (*Picks them up and puts them on the table.*) Okay...

JESS. Would you like a drink?

YVONNE. Er... Yes. Erm... A tea would be lovely, thanks. Milk and one sugar.

JESS. Oh, you'll have to make it. I can't. Sorry.

YVONNE. Of course. Yes… I should have offered.

JESS. No, it's fine.

YVONNE. Actually, I can go without. I've had four coffees already today! Is Flores a French name?

JESS. Spanish.

YVONNE. Oh… Tapas.

Awkward pause.

It's my first week doing this. All very new.

JESS. How's it going?

YVONNE. It's quite full-on. Some would say stressful… Okay, let's make a start… I'll be entering your answers into my laptop. They're multiple-choice questions. Now, there are two components. The daily living part and the mobility part.

JESS. Okay.

YVONNE. Can I confirm you have cerebral palsy?

JESS. Yes.

YVONNE. How long have you had it?

JESS. Pardon?

YVONNE. How long have you had your cerebral palsy?

JESS. All my life.

Beat.

You do know CP is nearly always from birth?

Awkward pause.

YVONNE.…. Yes. Course.

JESS. What's your background?

YVONNE.…. Sorry?

Beat.

Oh, you meant…

JESS. Last time I did this, I was six and I was awarded a lifelong benefit.

YVONNE. They… We don't do that any more.

JESS. Well, barring some kind of medical breakthrough, you don't really get better from CP…

YVONNE. Is there anything you'd like to add about how your cerebral palsy affects you?

JESS. Well, it gets worse, like if I'm tired or stressed or ill. So what I can and can't do can fluctuate. I can be less coordinated, more shaky. But I don't have any health issues and I don't take any medication.

YVONNE *writes down* JESS*'s answers on her laptop.*

YVONNE. Thank you. Right… Moving on to the questions. The first section is about preparing food. Are you able to prepare and cook a simple meal unaided?

JESS. No.

YVONNE. You're unable to prepare any food even if you had aids or assistance?

JESS. Correct.

YVONNE. Can you explain why?

JESS. I get twitches, which means I don't have the control to prepare food, or pour a drink – or cereal!

YVONNE. Okay, next…

Her phone rings. She mutes it.

Sorry… I thought I'd… put it on silent. Right. This part is about taking nutrition. Can you manage to eat food by yourself or do you need some kind of assistance?

JESS. I need someone to cut up my food.

YVONNE. Okay. The next section… Are you able to wash and bathe unaided?

JESS. I need help getting in and out of the shower.

YVONNE. Now on to managing toilet needs. Can you manage toilet needs or incontinence yourself?

JESS. Yes.

YVONNE. Okay. Dressing and undressing. Can you dress or get undressed unaided?

JESS. Not really.

YVONNE. What do you struggle with particularly? And why?

JESS. I can't do buttons or zips. And I find socks difficult…

YVONNE*'s work phone rings. This time she checks who it is.*

YVONNE. Er, work. I have to take this, sorry. My boss. (*Into phone*.) Hi, Keith… No… Well, maybe half an hour… But… Okay, yes, I'll try… yes… Bye. (*Looks upset*.) Erm… sorry.

JESS. Are you okay?

YVONNE. Apparently I'm supposed to be in Potters Bar now!

JESS. Do you need to…?

YVONNE *rushes through the next questions.*

YVONNE. So, you… you need assistance dressing and undressing if there are buttons or zips?

JESS. Yes, basically, I…

YVONNE. Okay, that's the daily living component completed. Next is the mobility component. We'll start with… Can you stand and then walk more than two hundred metres, either aided or unaided?

JESS. No.

YVONNE. Can you stand and then walk more than fifty metres but no more than two hundred metres, either aided or unaided?

JESS. No.

YVONNE. Can you stand and then walk unaided more than twenty metres but no more than fifty metres?

JESS. No.

YVONNE. Can you stand and then walk using an aid or appliance more than twenty metres but no more than fifty metres? (*Waits*.) Jessica?

JESS. Yeah, I can walk short distances if I take someone's arm.

YVONNE. Great.

JESS. I just want to add I can't use public transport on my own, so my Motability car's a big help. It allows me to commute to work, and have a life. (*Clears her throat*.) Would you mind holding up that water for me?

YVONNE. Er, yes, of course.

JESS takes a sip. YVONNE checks her watch nervously.

Scene Three

Therapy room. JESS sits in her armchair. She checks her watch. She waits.

AIDAN pops his head in. He is in his late thirties and has a sensitive, intelligent face. There is a lot bubbling under the surface. JESS waves him in.

JESS. Hi, come in.

AIDAN. My mistake!

He holds his hand up and starts to leave.

JESS. Who are you looking for?

AIDAN. Jessica... the therapist?

JESS. You've found her.

She smiles and holds out her hand. AIDAN *looks taken aback.*

Is there a problem?

AIDAN. No.

AIDAN *walks in. They shake hands.*

JESS. Good to meet you, Aidan.

AIDAN. Jessica.

JESS. People call me Jess. Sit down.

AIDAN *remains standing.*

AIDAN. I'm late. How late?

JESS. Half an hour.

AIDAN. I should just go.

JESS. We have twenty minutes.

AIDAN (*looks around the room*). Where's the couch? Isn't that the rule? Don't I lie down on a velvet thing and reveal how I've secretly always fancied my mother?

JESS. Ah, yes. While I stroke my beard and look pensive?

Beat. AIDAN *sits down.*

AIDAN. I nearly didn't come… How does this work? I talk, you cure me, and I live happily ever after?

JESS. We talk and we see what happens.

AIDAN. Customer satisfaction not guaranteed. At least you're honest.

He stares at JESS.

I'll be honest too. I have to be here. I'm not here because I want to be.

JESS. Okay.

AIDAN. They said I had to come here. That's the rule, apparently.

JESS. How long have you been there?

AIDAN. Four weeks and two days – like you don't know.

JESS. How are you finding it?

AIDAN *laughs bitterly.*

AIDAN. Oh, I just love it. Highlight of my life. You should try it…

JESS. Did you choose to go?

AIDAN. Yes. But I didn't choose to come here.

JESS. Why not?

AIDAN. I don't think moaning to a paid stranger is the solution to my problems.

JESS. Because?

AIDAN. It's self-indulgent, and being an alcoholic is self-indulgent enough. I have that box well and truly ticked already.

JESS. Have you had therapy before?

AIDAN. God, no. I'm only here because it's a 'rule' of rehab.

JESS. Then how do you know it won't help?

AIDAN. I think it's a money-spinner for people like you.

JESS. I see.

AIDAN. Yep. Without people like me, you wouldn't be in a job, would you?

JESS. No. And I wouldn't have my super-yacht!

They stare at each other.

AIDAN. I didn't expect my therapist to be disabled.

JESS. Why would you?

AIDAN. Cerebral palsy?

JESS. I prefer wobbly.

AIDAN. I thought you were drunk when I first saw you.

JESS. You're not the first. Last week I was getting into my car, and a very irate cabbie told me not to drink and drive.

    AIDAN *smiles fleetingly.*

AIDAN. You drive?

JESS. Yes. Can you?

AIDAN. No.

JESS. Any other questions?

AIDAN. Am I free to leave?

JESS. You are.

AIDAN. You won't stop me?

JESS. I don't do rugby tackles.

AIDAN. Can I have some water?

    JESS *invites him with a gesture of her hand to help himself to the jug of water and glass on the table next to her.*

    Beat.

JESS. Oh, I can't pour it for you. Sorry.

    AIDAN *pours himself some water.*

AIDAN. Are you just making up for centuries of patriarchy?

JESS. Got me again!

AIDAN (*sits down*). Why did you want to be a therapist?

JESS. I just really wanted a yacht.

AIDAN. I don't have to tell you anything.

JESS. No, you don't.

AIDAN. Whatever the rules say.

JESS. What do they say?

AIDAN. I'm quite happy to sit here in silence.

JESS. So am I.

AIDAN. Course, you still get paid. Win-win, right?

They sit in silence. AIDAN *fidgets.*

Do most people just come in here and start talking?

JESS. Depends.

AIDAN. No chit-chat? No moaning about the Tube? Or the weather or who won *Bake Off*?

JESS. Is that what you'd like to do?

AIDAN. I don't watch TV… I could moan about the Northern Line if you like.

JESS. Go for it.

AIDAN. Well, it never, ever runs on time. Always delayed. Like clockwork. Ironically.

They sit in silence again. AIDAN *checks his phone, then puts it back in his pocket.*

All this sun. I mean, this is Britain. It should be grey. That's the rule, you know.

JESS. Don't you like the sun?

AIDAN. No.

JESS. Why not?

AIDAN. Reminds me of the summer holidays.

JESS. Weren't they a happy time?

AIDAN. Not in my house.

JESS. Because…?

AIDAN (*waggles his finger at* JESS). Now, now. Do you always try to steer the conversation in such a crass way?

JESS. Do you always use humour to avoid talking about how you feel?

AIDAN. Yes. I find it's a handy emotional crutch and one that's served me very well over the years.

JESS. Crutches can be useful up to a point.

AIDAN. Says the wobbly girl... Is it hard being wobbly?

JESS. It has some challenges.

AIDAN. Like what?

JESS. I can't do certain things like... washing up.

AIDAN. Unless you worked in a Greek restaurant... Do you wish you were normal?

JESS. What's normal?

AIDAN. Actually, I worked in a Greek restaurant once. I was seventeen. Wanted to go to India like every other white, spotty brat. What a cliché.

JESS. Did you go?

AIDAN. Yes... but I flew home a week later.

JESS. Why?

AIDAN. My mum died... Is that what you call a juicy nugget?

JESS. What happened?

AIDAN. She had a brain bleed in the shower one morning. Dropped dead. Just like that.

JESS. That must have been such a shock.

AIDAN. Well done for pulling that titbit out of me.

JESS. I'm on your side, Aidan. I'm not trying to catch you out.

AIDAN. This isn't some schmaltzy American TV crap where you help me confront my pain.

JESS. So you do watch TV?

AIDAN. Only when I'm drunk... Do you treat a lot of alcoholics?

JESS. I see a few patients who engage in compulsive behaviours.

AIDAN. Now, there's a fancy name for 'pisshead'.

JESS. Actually, I prefer 'addicts'. Fewer syllables.

AIDAN. That's why you shorten your name. Energy-saving. Gotta save it up to deal with intransigent fuckers like me.

JESS. I wouldn't say that.

AIDAN. No?

JESS. Too many syllables.

Beat.

AIDAN. My parents were rich, you know. Rich and cold. Classic combo. I'm guessing you want me to sit here and gush about how hard my life has been as a poor little rich boy?

JESS. Do you believe that people who grow up in well-off families are immune to suffering?

AIDAN. I believe a poor, brown kid stitching trainers for ten p a day would tell me to grow a pair.

JESS. People are complex… If we don't get the care or attention we need as a child, it can cause real problems. Whether your parents have money or not is irrelevant.

AIDAN. Look at me. I'm a white, able-bodied, straight bloke. I'm privileged, whatever you say.

JESS. Privileged?

AIDAN. I grew up in a big house. Never went hungry or cold. Had lots of stuff. Room full of toys. A shiny bike.

JESS. What about what you didn't have?

She waits for him to answer.

Aidan, what about what you didn't –

AIDAN. Like a dad who gave a shit? (*Checks his watch.*) Well, I'll let you know if I can make next week. Being a pisshead is a time-consuming business. Thanks, Jess. It's been a blast.

AIDAN *gets up, pats* JESS*'s chair and walks out. She stares after him.*

Scene Four

JESS*'s living room/kitchen.* JESS *is cycling on the exercise bike.*

NADIA *enters.*

NADIA. Cześć! Hope you don't mind. I brought Poppy over...

JESS. But I'm not... (*Spots* POPPY.) Hey!

> POPPY *is a small woman in her early twenties, dressed in punky clothes. She has several piercings and tattoos. She uses an electric wheelchair and speaks with a northern accent.*

POPPY. You look normal on that thing. It's hilarious!

NADIA. She's right! You do. (*Clears up the kitchen table.*)

POPPY. I wish I bloody liked exercise! I'm more into biscuits.

JESS. I only use this when I'm angry!

NADIA. You never get angry, Jess!

JESS. Well, I was on the phone and I was put on hold for ages. Then someone cut me off!

POPPY. Happens to me a lot! (*To* NADIA.) Got any nibbles? And none of that healthy snack shite!

NADIA. Yes... (*Looks in her bag.*) Yep, these are terrible! Here you go.

> NADIA *opens a bag of crisps and gives them to* POPPY, *who starts eating.*

Have fun! I have to pick up Kuba.

JESS. What...?   POPPY. Give him a big
                                  smooch from me.

JESS *looks unsure about* NADIA *going.*

Okay...   Bye, Nads.

NADIA *blows a kiss to the girls and rushes off.*

POPPY. This is like a crip playdate, innit? It's like we met on Crinder! (*Laughs.*) Er... Hang on. Where's the telly? Wait. Is that a... ra-di-o? Holy shit! I'm gonna need some booze.

JESS. Well, I'd offer you a drink but I can't pour it.

POPPY. Or you're just a stingy bitch! (*Laughs a dirty laugh.*) I don't really do chit-chat – in case you hadn't noticed. Life's too short. Like me. First things first, who's that hot guy I've seen coming here? Dark hair. Glasses.

JESS. Adam?

POPPY. You shagging him?... That's a yes, then... You're proper blushing!

JESS. I was seeing him for a bit.

POPPY. You say seeing. I say shagging.

JESS. I hate that word!

POPPY. What's wrong with it?

JESS. It's so... unromantic! Like a hairy carpet!

POPPY. Don't knock a hairy carpet! Some men love 'em! (*Laughs.*) You a romantic, then? Parents still married, are they?

JESS. Forty years.

POPPY. Pass the bucket! (*Laughs.*) I ain't seen my dad since I was fourteen. They local?

JESS. Yeah, but they're in Spain now, looking after my gran. Dementia.

POPPY. Nads said you got a brother. Where is he?

JESS. Mexico. Travelling.

POPPY. Always wanted a brother. But it's just me. Dad left Mum when I was two. Shagged around like a sailor. You really think true love exists? Not on Tinder, then?

JESS. No way.

JESS *gets off the bike and stretches out.*

POPPY. I am. I've had some well good nights courtesy of
Tinder! And mornings. And afternoons! I bloody love this
city, I do.

JESS. Where did you grow up?

POPPY. Tiny village up north. 'Butt-fuck-nowhere-ville' I call it.
Mum couldn't cope with my 'terrible affliction' so I moved
there to live with my grandparents when I was five. They're
dead now. They were well sweet but their idea of a wild night
was watching *Emmerdale* with a curry! I swear, I nearly slit
my wrists in that place. Then Nan found my vibrator one day
and it all went a bit south! Couldn't look me in the eye. You'd
be the same, eh?

JESS. Hey, I'm a romantic, not prudish!

POPPY. If you say so! Nads says you're a therapist. Nosy cow,
are ya?

JESS *nods.*

Bet people think you're just amazing, don't they?! 'Ooh,
she's wobbly and she's a therapist! Wow. She's so
inspirational!' (*Sticks her fingers down her throat.*) Yeurrgh!
I tell you what, I can't stand those motivational-speaker crips
who are like, 'I've got no arms and legs and I've just
climbed Mount Everest in a pair of flip-flops!' They make
me look like a right loser! And don't get me started on the
fucking Paralympics! I hated PE at school!... I bet you were
teacher's pet, weren't you? Did you go to a – (*In 'disabled'
voice.*) 'special' school?

JESS. Like Eton?

POPPY. Like the ones for 'poor, handicapped children'? The
'Handi-bin' we called it!

JESS. No, I went to a 'normal' all-girls school. It was... What's
the word? Shit.

POPPY. Mine was shit too. Staff were fucking patronising! When
we hit sixteen, we had to fight for the right to choose what we

ate for lunch. My best mate, Baz – he's more wobbly than you and in a chair. One day he said to his helper, 'If I have to eat another boiled carrot, I'm gonna shove it up your arse!' Treated us like morons. Had no idea we were getting high and copping off with each other! Baz used to scope us loadsa ganj. Don't know how we'd have survived otherwise. Baz is such a rebel, like me. Live fast, die young!

JESS. What's he doing now?

POPPY. Living in a fucking care home for oldies. Because there's no 'suitable properties' where he lives... It's criminal! They treat him like a five-year-old. That's what he can't stand...

JESS. God, that would make me angry.

POPPY. Nads said you don't get angry. Or have rows.

JESS. Well, I try not to. I don't see the point.

POPPY. Oh, there's a massive point. Honestly, some of the best moments of my life have come from a perfectly timed 'Fuck you!' I love a good barney! Gets the endorphins going, donnit?... You know, I've met crips like you, 'I have to make up for being disabled by always being nice cos, if I want to be accepted, I have to be like the Dalai fucking Lama.'

Beat.

JESS. Fuck you!

POPPY. That's my girl! Let your inner bitch out. That's proper equality, innit? The right to go full-on mental sometimes. Let out the wobbly RAAAGE!

JESS throws a crumpled-up letter at POPPY. *It misses by a mile.* POPPY *laughs.*

Well, your inner bitch throws like a drunk!... I bet you don't even drink?! Great! Nads has dumped me with a teetotal nun who has a fucking radio. Shoot me in the face, please!... (*Laughs.*) I ain't got time for this! You know, I finally moved down here, then, bang, Covid hit and my GP told me to 'shield' for blooming eternity. Went up the walls with boredom! Thank fuck for Tinder! I'm back out there now but everything's so steep, ain't it? I mean, I had, like, four quid in my account last month after bills. And I don't buy, like, anything! But I want to take singing lessons. That's my dream, that is, to maybe teach singing one day… (*Spots a letter on the table.*) Nads said you had your PIP assessment a while ago? What happened?

JESS. Okay, don't tell her… They took me off the higher rate of Mobility but I'm appealing it. And I'm pretty sure I'll win. It's a mistake, I think. She was new.

POPPY. Mistake my arse! I did my PIP last year. Got the same rate as before. But they keep trying to find me 'fit for work'. Thing is, I have chronic pain in my joints so most jobs are out. Irony is, I want to bloody work. I don't want to sit at home all day watching *Bargain* bleedin' *Hunt*. But, hey ho, they got to do their thing. Know what my latest drama is? Drum roll… Council's cut my night-time care. Completely! And I can't afford private. So now I have to be in bed by nine, for fuck's sake! Nine! Put a right spanner in my social life, it has.

JESS. Are you appealing?

POPPY. Shit, yeah!

JESS. Good.

POPPY. I'm not letting them twats ruin my life. I even wrote to our MP last week. Oliver Har-something! So not me. God, I bore the tits off myself sometimes, always going on about flipping benefits, carers, yada-yada. I just want to get on with life. But, the minute I do, wham! A new fight… I mean, it's using up precious time when I could be…

JESS. …on Tinder?

POPPY. Exactly! I just want to have fun. Like any other young bint. Is that too much to ask?

JESS. No. You have every right to want that.

POPPY. If I had a drink, I'd raise my glass to you.

JESS (*mimes raising a glass*). Clink.

POPPY (*mimes clinking* JESS*'s glass*). Clink!

Scene Five

Therapy room. JESS *and* RITA *sit opposite each other.*

JESS. I'll see you on Monday.

RITA. Yeah, about that… Erm… I'm going to have to stop for a bit. I don't want to. I'm sorry.

JESS. Don't apologise. Maybe we could try –

RITA. I can't afford it right now. I missed an appointment at the Jobcentre and it all… (*Mimes an explosion.*) Sorry, I shouldn't be burdening you with… (*Trails off.*)

JESS. Have you got someone who can help you through this?

RITA. My cousin, Trish. She's a trooper. Lends me money. Brings me food when I can't leave the house… Aah… (*Composes herself.*) Bit teary, there! I'm seeing my doctor next week. I'm hoping she'll be able to help with the Jobcentre people.

JESS. You know where I am.

RITA. Thank you. And thanks for giving me a reduced rate. (*Gets emotional.*) I can't tell you what that means to me. I don't really do hugs but am I allowed to try? I'll try just putting my arms around you, if that's okay?

JESS. Course. Keep it a secret!

RITA *mimes sealing her lips.*

JESS *stands up and* RITA *tentatively puts her arms around her.*

AIDAN *enters. He is carrying a near-empty bottle of vodka.* RITA *jumps back from the hug with* JESS.

AIDAN. Knock, knock!

He waves the bottle at JESS.

RITA (*to* JESS). Thank you. (*Agitated, to* AIDAN.) Can I get past?

AIDAN. Of course, m'lady.

Standing aside, he makes an exaggerated gesture to her.
RITA *edges past him and slips out.*

Remember me?

JESS *seems wary of the state* AIDAN *is in.*

Sorry I haven't come in a while. I was… feeling very, very
sorry for myself. Nothing personal. You know that.

JESS. Have you been drinking?

AIDAN. Well, it's lovely to see you too!

Beat.

Is this in violation of the rules? Are you going to strike me
off as a patient?

JESS. Do you want me to?

AIDAN. I didn't know where else to go… Now surely that's an
ego boost…? Can I sit here for a bit?

JESS. Aidan, I'm leaving.

She drops to her knees and shuffles towards the door.

AIDAN. Wait!

JESS *stops.* AIDAN *walks over to the door and blocks it.*
JESS *looks nervous.*

Can I show you a photo?

JESS *doesn't move.* AIDAN *takes out an old photo and
holds it up to* JESS. *She looks at it, still wary of* AIDAN.

This is Maeve. Maeve O'Reilly… That's me. All skin and
bone. I was always eating but you'd never know. Maeve's all
round. Look at her. Round and soft. I used to sit on her lap
and she'd say – (*In Irish accent.*) 'Jaysus, you've got a bony
little rump, haven't ya?!'

JESS. Who's Maeve?

AIDAN. She brought me up.

JESS. Your nanny?

AIDAN. I hate that word!... I just called her Maeve. I thought all kids had a Maeve. All kids should have a Maeve.

JESS. What age were you when she arrived?

AIDAN. Six months or so, I think. She was always there.

AIDAN puts the photo away and walks away from JESS.

I shouldn't have come here. It was rude of me to just turn up.

JESS. Where was Maeve from?

AIDAN. Dublin. She had a little cottage near the canal. It was damp and cramped and the taps wouldn't stop dripping. I loved it... Maeve never touched a drop of drink. She called it the devil's tipple. Her husband died of liver failure. It would break her heart to know I'm...

AIDAN slumps into a chair. JESS shuffles a bit closer to him.

JESS. Did she live with you here?

AIDAN. Yes. She had a small room next to mine.

Beat.

It smelt different to the rest of the house. Like her. Soap and oranges... Maeve loved oranges. She told me she used to get an orange for Christmas as a kid. Just one orange a year. She couldn't believe her luck when she found out she could eat one every day. She'd always have a bowl of them by her bed. We'd sit side by side and she'd peel one with her hands. She didn't like using a knife. Said they were too special to cut open, that they needed to be handled with care. Then she'd give me a piece and she'd eat the next. It was our ritual. Every day after school. She'd make up stories about where it had come from, who had picked it and how far it had travelled to reach me. She was a great storyteller. I loved listening to her voice. It was strong and warm. Like her. On my birthday, she'd bake me an orange cake... My parents didn't really do birthdays. Fusses were frowned upon. But, Maeve, she was all about the fuss... She used to stand over me as I ate her cake, like an old guard dog. I felt smothered in love.

He registers JESS *for the first time in a while.*

Did you have someone like that?

JESS. Yes. I did.

AIDAN. Good. I never really saw my mum much… Dad didn't
like Maeve. Said she mollycoddled me. He told her to leave
when I turned thirteen… Mum would have let her stay. She
never put her foot down about anything. Hated 'scenes'…
I came home from school one day and Maeve was gone.
She'd left a bowl of oranges on my bed. (*Laughs scornfully.*)
What a woeful tale of the little rich boy losing his beloved
nanny. Pathetic, huh? 'Pull yourself together, man!'… I slept
in her bed for six weeks. Until Dad found out and locked the
door to her room… Anyway, enough about me. How have
you been? I'm sorry for not turning up before now.

JESS. It's your choice whether to come or not.

AIDAN. Because I'm an adult?

AIDAN *slides off his chair onto the floor. He grips the
bottle.*

Maeve would tell me not to drink this.

JESS. Did you see her after she left?

AIDAN. Not for years. She moved back to Dublin. I wrote to
her every Saturday. You know, I started drinking heavily
when she died. Never clocked that before now… Fitting
tribute to her if ever there was one.

He raises the bottle in the air, then lowers it onto his lap.

Five years ago it was. I was so angry at my father. Didn't
even come to the funeral. I sat there on my own in that little
cold church, crying my eyes out. All I could think of was
him telling me to 'man up'… I was never allowed to… He's
not one for anything 'messy'.

JESS *moves a bit closer to* AIDAN.

JESS. What do you mean by 'messy'?

AIDAN. Anything he can't control. You know what, I think I'm scared of messy too. We do have something in common. Fancy that? (*Chuckles*.) So, here's a tale for you. He told me once... that he fell off a horse when he was sixteen. Broke his leg badly. He was lying in hospital with his leg in a cast, and the doctor told him he wouldn't be able to walk for four months. His father leaned over and whispered, 'Prove him wrong, walk in three!' And he did... He told me that the last time I saw him. Three years ago... His little prelude to telling me to 'get my act together' and 'stop drinking'. He has no time for indulging people. Mind over matter and all that. That's what he was taught. That's what he believes. Those are the rules.

JESS. You mention rules a lot.

AIDAN. Do I? My father's a big fan of rules. Says they give life order and structure.

JESS. What do you think?

AIDAN. He likes rules because he's a cunt.

He takes out an orange and peels it, carefully, with his fingers.

It's my birthday today.

He eats a segment of orange then offers one to JESS. *She takes it. They sit together in silence.*

Scene Six

JESS's living room/kitchen. NADIA rushes in. She is soaking wet.

JESS. Hey. You're all wet!

NADIA. Cześć!... I forgot my umbrella. Of all the days! Monsoon rain out there!

JESS. Oh, no!

NADIA. I can't imagine what I look like now... Keep me away from mirrors!

NADIA laughs and pats her hair.

Okay... Lunch!

JESS. How about the yummy curry in the freezer?

NADIA. No, no time to de-freeze that! Sorry, Kochana! I brought you cheese sandwich. That okay?

JESS. Fine. Yeah.

NADIA takes the sandwich out of her bag and sets it down on the table.

NADIA. Ah, what a week it's been! My poor feet. I have big plans tonight. Oh, yes... Me, a bottle of wine and Mr Lionel Richie!

She dances a little, singing the words to 'All Night Long' as she folds some clean laundry.

JESS watches her.

JESS. Have I ever told you how much I love your coordination? It's a thing of great beauty!

NADIA. Nobody's told me that before!

JESS. It is! You probably don't even appreciate it but you should.

NADIA. You make me laugh, Jess! What else should I appreciate then? Tell me.

JESS. Well, this may sound weird but I was just thinking, 'I'm so glad I don't have a toothache right now!' And, suddenly, I felt so happy! So... Not being in pain!

NADIA. Well, I'll try and remember to do that next time I'm standing on a bus with someone's unwashed armpit stuck in my face! Jess, I barely remember my own name these days. It's just rush, rush, rush. All since council's cut our time with our clients!

JESS. I hate that word. 'Client.' Eurrgh!

NADIA. You make me laugh!

JESS. 'Client' is such a bullshit term.

NADIA. What do you call the people who come to you?

JESS. Patients. Not clients.

NADIA. What should I call you then?

JESS. Jess will do.

NADIA. No! In general. I spend my day helping... Who?... Service users?

JESS (*in a robot voice*). I. Am. A. Service. User.

NADIA (*laughs*). Okay... So what then?

JESS. Erm... People?

NADIA. People?

JESS. Yep. Old-school. What's people in Polish?

NADIA. Ludzi.

JESS. Ludzi. Perfect.

NADIA. Whatever they make us call you, there's never enough time. The worst thing is we look like bad guys. I'm doing my best. But, what can you do in fifteen minutes? It's just impossible...

JESS. It isn't your fault. You're doing a great job, Nads.

NADIA. Sorry, Jess. I moan every time I see you.

JESS. Moan away. It's my job, remember?

NADIA *composes herself and sits down next to* JESS.

NADIA. Ooh, did you hear about your PIP yet?

JESS. Not yet. No.

NADIA. God – he will help you. I know it. (*Pats* JESS*'s arm.*) Oh, I forgot to give you your sandwich! My so-tired brain! (*Jumps up and gets the sandwich.*) I feel this is all I ever give you these days. Bad shop food. My mother would not approve! I should really clean up, but tick tock... Is Lottie back yet?

JESS. No, still at her mum's. Don't worry. I'll ask the carer later to clear up. Go!

NADIA. You're an angel! (*Puts her coat on.*) I'm still so angry they cut my hours with you!

JESS. Send him my love.

NADIA. Who?

JESS. Mr Richie!

NADIA. Darling, I'm gonna rock this wet coat, get on the Tube, and enjoy not having a toothache all the way to my next clients... Ludzi!

We hear NADIA*'s laughter as she leaves.* JESS *stares at her sandwich.*

Scene Seven

POPPY*'s studio flat. Shabby. Bare.* DOM, *a young black man, enters carrying* POPPY *in his arms. They have been clubbing, and are relaxed and happy. They sit on the floor.*

POPPY. Either this stuff is really good or I'm sitting next to Idris fucking Elba!

DOM. That brother ain't got nothing on me!

He leans over and kisses POPPY. *He lifts her onto his lap and she straddles him.*

You are so damn cute, girl. Like a... kitten!

POPPY. Me-ow!

DOM *kisses her neck and shoulders.* POPPY *moans in delight but then she moans in pain.*

DOM. You okay?

POPPY. Yeah, just my neck. It gives me agg sometimes!

DOM. We need a code for good moans and bad moans. I don't want to hurt you.

POPPY. Ooh, a true gentleman. Your mum brought you up proper, didn't she?

DOM. Damn right.

POPPY. Mummy's boy, are we?

DOM. Not cool, huh? But she's a real legend.

POPPY. I know. She made you.

She kisses his neck.

Are you really a mechanic? Or do you just say it because it sounds hot?

DOM. Fully qualified. Cross my heart!

POPPY. I have trust issues. I need more proof.

DOM. Oh, yeah. Like what?

POPPY. What's a connecting rod?

DOM *laughs.*

You don't know, do you?

DOM. It connects the piston to the crankshaft. How the hell do you know about connecting rods?

POPPY. My uncle was a mechanic. And I'm very interested in rods and shafts.

DOM. Are you now?

POPPY. I am. (*Stroking his chest.*) Do you own a pair of greasy overalls?

DOM. I feel very objectified by you right now!

POPPY. Good!

POPPY *presses the palms of her small hands against* DOM*'s.*

You have very big hands.

DOM. I do.

POPPY. I like a man with big hands. My hands are very small.

DOM *kisses her hands.*

And they make everything I hold look very big.

DOM. I like them even more. (*Pulls off his top.*) It's cold in here. You better warm me up.

They kiss and touch each other. It's noisy and playful. POPPY *moans with pleasure.*

POPPY. That's a good moan, by the way!…

DOM. Phew.

DOM *kisses her neck.*

POPPY. Good… Good… Aah… No… fucking amazing!

Cradling POPPY *in his arms,* DOM *carries her off.*

Scene Eight

JESS's *living room/kitchen. The next morning. Dirty dishes and glasses are piled high on the table.* JESS *is wearing the same clothes as in Scene Six. She shuffles on her knees to the kitchen table to sip some water but knocks over a glass. It falls to the floor and smashes.* JESS *recoils and steps back onto a piece of the glass.*

JESS. Ow!

> *She drops to her knees again, removes her sock, and dabs her bleeding foot with tissues. Leaving the bloody tissues on the floor, she crawls to the sofa.*

> LOTTIE *enters, pulling a suitcase behind her. She holds up her hand apologetically.*

LOTTIE. I know, I know, I'm late. Not my fault though. Crappy trains!

> *She peels off her coat, bag, shoes and jumper, and dumps them on the floor.*

Aah, I've missed you so much…

JESS. You are always late.

LOTTIE. No. Not always!

JESS. Yes, always. You're punctuality-challenged. (*Jokingly.*) Were you born like that?

LOTTIE. Was 'punctuality-challenged' hard for you to say?

> JESS *gives her the finger.* LOTTIE *walks over to her and they hug.*

Back at last! Feels like I've been away forever.

> LOTTIE *flops down on the sofa.*

Dad just called. Did my head in. Just when I was decompressing after weeks of Mum doing my head in! Jeez, I wish I had your parents.

JESS. Have you told him yet?

LOTTIE. Don't give me that face! So, before you ask, I can now officially confirm me and Mum are not cut out to spend that much time together! God, I'm such a dick! She's practically dying and here I am, still moaning about her.

JESS. Fancy a cuppa?

LOTTIE *laughs*.

What?

LOTTIE. You never just say 'Can I have a cuppa, Lottie?'! You always say 'Do you want a cuppa?' or 'Shall we have a cuppa?'

JESS. No, I don't!

LOTTIE. Yes, you do. Ever since I've known you!

JESS *is lost for words*.

Just bloody ask me! It's not a big deal.

JESS. I know it isn't.

LOTTIE. So just ask me directly, then!

JESS. Get me a cuppa, bitch!

LOTTIE (*with feigned shock*). Ooh, you demanding cow!

LOTTIE *walks over to the kitchen area*.

Why's there such a mess?

JESS. The carer didn't turn up last night.

LOTTIE. Bloody hell! Not again!… So you didn't eat dinner?

JESS. Yeah, I knocked up some wild mushroom gnocchi with parmesan shavings.

LOTTIE. Jess? So you haven't eaten since…?

JESS. About four yesterday.

LOTTIE. Holy crap, that's like… a day ago!! You should have told me the second I got here instead of letting me chew your ear off!

LOTTIE *notices the bloody tissues on the floor.*

Oh my God, is that blood? What happened?

JESS. Iain Duncan Smith came by. I killed him.

LOTTIE. Jess!

JESS. I broke a glass and stood on it.

LOTTIE. Shit! You didn't tell me that either! Jess… Let me look at your foot.

She hurries over to inspect JESS*'s foot.*

Babe, that does not look good. I think you still have something wedged in it. Does it hurt?

JESS. A bit.

LOTTIE. I can't get that out. We're gonna have to go to A&E.

JESS. Ah no!

LOTTIE. Come on. I'll drive us. Where are the car keys?

She waits for an answer.

Hello?

JESS. I…

LOTTIE. What?

JESS. …Lost the car.

LOTTIE. What? When?!

JESS. Last week. They took it.

LOTTIE. Who took it?

JESS. Motability.

LOTTIE. What happened?!

JESS. I didn't qualify for the higher Mobility rate.

LOTTIE. Can you get it back?

JESS. Course I will.

LOTTIE. When?

JESS. They turned down my first appeal so now I have to wait for a tribunal.

LOTTIE. That sounds scary. Why didn't you qualify for the higher rate?

JESS. I think it's because I said I could walk twenty metres with help. I was too honest, apparently.

LOTTIE. How are you getting to work and stuff?

JESS. Taxis.

LOTTIE. How are you affording that?

JESS. Well, they've given me two grand towards a new car but my adaptations alone cost loads so...

LOTTIE. Have you written to your MP?

JESS. Oliver Hargreaves? Mr 'Just Be Patient'? Oh, yeah...

JESS winces.

LOTTIE. Okay, I'm going to... get us a cab and bandage your foot. Then make you food.

LOTTIE takes out her mobile and books a cab.

JESS. Sorry.

LOTTIE. This is sheer bliss compared to Mum's. Trust me.

LOTTIE rummages through her bag and pulls out a sanitary pad.

JESS. I am not putting a sanitary pad on my foot!

LOTTIE. We're doing this.

She places JESS's foot on her lap. It twitches.

Is that your...?

JESS. CP twitch. Yeah!

JESS's foot twitches again.

I need to think of something else.

LOTTIE. Like when guys think of stuff to stop them coming?

JESS. Exactly!

LOTTIE. Why didn't you ring me last night?

JESS. You were three hours away! Plus, you're my friend not my carer.

LOTTIE. Friends care for each other! (*Phone beeps.*) Ooh, taxi's here! We'll grab you some food on the way. Come on.

LOTTIE helps JESS to her feet.

Scene Nine

Hospital room. JESS and LOTTIE wait.

LOTTIE (*pacing the floor*). I know the NHS is fucked but this is taking the piss! Covid or no Covid! How long have…

She stops when DR ANDERSON, a female doctor, enters. She speaks with a Scottish accent and looks exhausted.

DR ANDERSON. Hi.

JESS. Hi.

DR ANDERSON (*to LOTTIE*). I'm Dr Anderson. Sorry for the long wait… Mad today. What's happened?

LOTTIE looks at JESS.

JESS. I stepped on some glass.

DR ANDERSON. Okay. Can she show me her foot, please?

LOTTIE (*loudly to JESS, as if she were deaf*). The lady would like you to show her your foot.

DR ANDERSON. Sorry. Can you put your foot on my lap, please?

JESS places her foot on DR ANDERSON's lap.

LOTTIE. She's a doctor too, you know.

DR ANDERSON. Pardon?

LOTTIE. She's a doctor.

DR ANDERSON *stares at* JESS.

JESS. She means I have a PhD.

DR ANDERSON. In medicine?

JESS. Psychology.

DR ANDERSON. Good for you.

JESS*'s foot twitches*.

JESS. Sorry. It twitches.

DR ANDERSON. Cerebral palsy, is it?

JESS. I say wobbly.

DR ANDERSON *looks confused*.

Have you tried putting 'cerebral palsy' on Tinder?

LOTTIE *stifles a laugh*.

DR ANDERSON. Okay. Well, there does seem to be a foreign body lodged in there. I should be able to pull it out and patch it up.

She reaches for some tweezers and sets about removing the shard of glass from JESS*'s foot*.

JESS (*winces*). How long will it take to heal?

DR ANDERSON. Maybe a week or so. You should try and keep the weight off it if possible.

JESS. Okay. I'm kind of stuck inside anyway right now.

LOTTIE. They took her Motability car back. The government.

DR ANDERSON. Oh, do you drive?

JESS. Yes, when I had a car.

DR ANDERSON. Well done.

JESS. And I've only killed two people.

Scene Ten

Therapy room. JESS *is on her phone waiting to talk to someone. She takes a sip of water.*

JESS. Yes, I phoned last week... I want to know how long before I get a date for my tribunal... So, basically, you don't know?... What does that mean?... Okay... Thanks.

She hangs up and is about to make another call when AIDAN *walks in.*

AIDAN. Hi.

JESS. Hi.

He sits down opposite her.

How are you?

AIDAN. Okay.

JESS. I wasn't sure you'd come.

AIDAN shrugs. They sit in silence.

AIDAN. I hope you don't think we had some kind of breakthrough because of last time... I didn't know what I was saying. I mean, I know it was some self-pitying bullshit and I apologise profusely. But I'm not going to subject you to that again.

JESS. Why are you here then?

AIDAN. I wanted to come and end our sessions formally. I thought you deserved that.

JESS. That's a shame.

AIDAN. Isn't it a relief?

JESS. Why?

AIDAN. Because I'm hardly a model patient.

JESS. What's a model patient?

AIDAN. Someone who doesn't turn up unannounced and forces you to eat an orange.

JESS. You turned up because you needed to talk. I was glad you did.

AIDAN. I turned up because I was in a rut and I do stupid things when I'm in a rut.

JESS. Do you think coming here was stupid?

AIDAN. Yes. Very stupid.

JESS. Why?

AIDAN. Because you don't care about me. You talk to me because you're paid to.

JESS. So if someone is paid, it means they can't genuinely care about you?

AIDAN. Spot on.

JESS. What about Maeve?

Beat.

AIDAN. That's different.

JESS. How so?

AIDAN. Do you care about me?

JESS. Yes.

AIDAN. Touching.

JESS. Is that hard for you to hear?

AIDAN. What?

JESS. That I care about you.

AIDAN. You think I have trust issues. Fine. Okay. Is this where it's going?

JESS. Do you have friends? Are you in a relationship?

AIDAN. Fuck you.

AIDAN *walks to the door, opens it, then shuts it.*

So do you think I have trust issues?

JESS. I think you're nervous about trusting me.

AIDAN. Why's that, then?

JESS. Because Maeve left you when you were thirteen. Your mum died when you were seventeen. And your father couldn't love you the way you needed him to. The three most important people in your life abandoned you in some way.

AIDAN. My father couldn't love me the way I needed him to. Hmmm. Interesting take on it.

JESS. What's your take?

AIDAN. I don't want to talk about him. You wouldn't either if you knew him. You'd despise him too.

JESS. Why?

AIDAN. By your reasoning, I'm the weak, pathetic little victim in all of this?

JESS. You're here. There's nothing weak or pathetic about that.

AIDAN. You know what I think?… I think how do you know what it's like to be me? By the looks of it, you've had a pretty rosy life. Yeah, okay, you're a bit wobbly but I bet you had a wonderful family who doted on you and gave you all the love and attention you could ever need. I bet you all hang out together, not because you have to, oh no, but because you actually want to. So don't pretend to have the answers to my problems because you haven't the faintest idea what it's like to be drowning in fucking pain all the time.

JESS. Look, there is no easy answer. But we can try and find a way through.

AIDAN. I don't want to find a way through.

JESS. Are you scared of trying?… Aidan…

AIDAN (*approaching* JESS). You're very sweet, but I'm not worth the bother. I'm a bitter, twisted, old soul. And you, you're one of those kind, naive folk who life hasn't fucked over yet. We are different animals, living in different universes.

JESS. We're all living in different universes.

AIDAN. Some are rosier than others.

JESS. You're right. I have had a loving family, but it hasn't all been rosy. I promise you.

Beat.

AIDAN. But I bet you don't feel like a piece of shit. Right here. (*Taps his chest.*) All the time. And I bet you don't have your dad's voice in your head, chip, chip, chipping away at you. And you know what kills me? That I still care about what the old bastard thinks of me. After all these years. It's fucking ridiculous!

JESS. Aidan. Don't stop coming here. We can get somewhere.

AIDAN. I can't. I'm not strong enough.

JESS. What would Maeve say?

AIDAN. Maeve was far stronger than I'll ever be.

He pats JESS *on the shoulder.*

You know where I am if you need me. Not that you will.

AIDAN *leaves.* JESS *stares after him.*

JESS. Fuck!

Scene Eleven

POPPY*'s flat. Music plays. She is in her wheelchair in a skimpy dress and heavy make-up. Smoking a spliff, she looks happy and stoned.* JESS *and* LOTTIE *enter.*

POPPY. Welcome, my homies... (*Waves them in.*) Come into my palace!

LOTTIE. Someone's had a good night. We brought a bag of chips with 'shitloads' of vinegar as the homie requested.

She hands POPPY *the bag of chips.* JESS *sits on the bed.*

POPPY. I got the munchies! (*Giggles.*) They smell soooo good!

POPPY *wolfs down the chips.* LOTTIE *takes off her coat and looks around for a place to hang it.*

Just dump it there... Not exactly *Grand Designs*, huh?

LOTTIE *dumps her jacket and bag on the floor.*

LOTTIE. Well, more... Shabby chic.

POPPY. That's posh for shithole!... Chips are well nice!... So, I hooked up with a guy... American dude. Great kisser! Well fit. You missed him by about half an hour.

JESS. He came back here?

POPPY. No, he promised to write to my father and ask for my hand in marriage... Course he fucking came back here!

LOTTIE *laughs.*

No action though. His girlfriend called and he scarpered. Toke?

She offers LOTTIE *her spliff.*

LOTTIE. A tiny puff. (*Takes the spliff.*) Whoa, that's strong! You must be high as kite.

POPPY. Only kind of high I'll ever be... Jess?

JESS. No, thanks.

POPPY. Go on, it might make you walk in a straight line!

LOTTIE. Jess isn't a fan.

POPPY. Course she isn't.

LOTTIE *gives the spliff back to* POPPY.

LOTTIE. She tried rolling a joint once but she dropped half of it on the floor!

POPPY. You should have rolled up the carpet and smoked that, ha! It would have been the world's biggest joint!...

JESS. It's freezing in here!

POPPY. Don't be such a wuss! You southerners! I'm trying to keep the bills down, aren't I? So I can go out. (*Rubs her head.*) Ooh, my head! I'm a woozy floozy... You girls should have come with me. Next time! We need to fix Jess up. She needs a shag!

LOTTIE. How do we do this, then?

POPPY. What?

LOTTIE. Get you into bed.

POPPY. I'm still eating my chips. Let's hang first!

LOTTIE. Gotta be up at seven! Work.

POPPY. Where do you work, then?

LOTTIE. I'm temping. PR company.

POPPY. Is it full of cunts? I know what that lot are like. Pretentious bastards. All 'Ooh, have some canapés and sushi' while spouting bullshit! Why the fuck you working there?

LOTTIE. I'm trying to work out what I want to do! We can't all love our jobs.

POPPY. Jess does. My grandpa was a security guard for forty-four years. Hated every day. His boss didn't even come to his funeral. Don't settle for shit. It's my mantra! (*Crumples up the bag of chips.*) Okay, I've hit my limit!

LOTTIE *takes the bag of chips and puts it on the table.*

POPPY *has another toke.*

LOTTIE. So, come on, lady, what do I need to do?

POPPY. First. I've got something to ask you.

LOTTIE. O-kay...

POPPY. Don't you miss cock?

LOTTIE. What?!

POPPY. Jess says you're gay. Don't you miss cock?

LOTTIE. No!

JESS. Shall we get on –

POPPY (*to* LOTTIE). What did your folks say when you came out?

LOTTIE. Mum said she knew all along. She was fine, really.

POPPY. And your dad?... Hello?

LOTTIE. I haven't told him yet.

POPPY*'s eyes widen. She shakes her head in shock.*

He's... Look, where he's from, it's a big deal.

POPPY. Just tell him the truth. If he goes ape, that's his problem. Not yours.

LOTTIE. Much as I'm enjoying this chat, it's nearly three a.m. So...

POPPY (*stubs out the spliff and moves her chair closer to her bed*). Okay, put your arms under my armpits and I'll put my arms around your neck. Okay?

LOTTIE *follows* POPPY*'s instructions.*

Okay... I'm warning you. I'm heavy. I don't look it but I am!

LOTTIE *lifts* POPPY *onto the bed.*

LOTTIE. Bloody hell! Okay... What's next?

POPPY. Lottie, will you… (*Flirting*.) Take my dress off? There's a zip down the back. Just roll me over. You know you want to!

They laugh. LOTTIE *rolls* POPPY *over.*

LOTTIE. You're lucky I'm a dab hand at undressing women!

POPPY. Is it making you horny?

LOTTIE. Oh, yeah, baby!

They laugh. LOTTIE *pulls* POPPY'*s dress off.* POPPY *squeezes her boobs together.*

POPPY. I have got great tits, haven't I?

LOTTIE. They are pretty darn pert! Where's your PJs?

POPPY. In the drawer.

JESS *pulls open a drawer under the bed and passes a long Nirvana T-shirt to* LOTTIE.

LOTTIE. Love a bit of Kurt! Okay… There we go.

LOTTIE *puts the T-shirt on* POPPY, *who then lies back.*

POPPY. Now, the embarrassing bit.

LOTTIE. Hit me.

POPPY. I need you to take these knickers off, grab a nappy, and put it on me. Jess, can you handle that? Or are you gonna spontaneously combust at the sight of my noo-naa?

JESS *and* LOTTIE *laugh.*

LOTTIE. Your noo-naa?!

POPPY. Yeah! What do you call it?

LOTTIE. Chi-chi.

JESS *and* POPPY *laugh.*

POPPY. Sounds like a poodle…! What do you call it, Jess? One's – (*Adopts posh voice.*) 'lady parts'?

JESS. No!

POPPY. Go on! Tell us.

LOTTIE and POPPY *stare at* JESS *expectantly.*

JESS. Mrs Woo-Woo.

LOTTIE and POPPY *crack up.*

POPPY. Jesus Christ! Mrs Woo-Woo?!

LOTTIE. You never told me that!

POPPY. Bringing people closer. That's what I do!

LOTTIE. Where are they?

POPPY. Under the bed.

JESS looks in the drawer under the bed.

See them?

JESS. Yep.

JESS hands LOTTIE *an adult nappy.*

POPPY. Sexilicious, huh?

LOTTIE. Shall I take off your knickers?

POPPY. Well, since you asked so nicely! Ooh, I might be turning here. What's her name?

LOTTIE. Sam.

POPPY. Sam better watch out!

LOTTIE pulls off POPPY*'s knickers and puts the adult nappy on* POPPY.

Make sure you pull it up so it don't jiggle about.

LOTTIE carefully follows POPPY*'s instructions.*

(*Lying down again.*) You can leave those ones in the loo. Nads will sort them out tomorrow.

LOTTIE. No probs. Can I use the loo?

POPPY. Course. Don't want you pissing yourself. That's my job!

LOTTIE *takes* POPPY*'s knickers and disappears to the loo.*

JESS. You look cold.

JESS *covers* POPPY *with the duvet.*

POPPY. Ta. For arranging all this. Don't know what I'd do without you. Mrs Woo-woo!

JESS. Shut up!… When will you hear if you're getting your night hours back?

POPPY. Any day now. I'm dreading it… Feels like I'm always waiting. I hate waiting. Done so much of it.

JESS. I know.

Beat.

POPPY. Have you told Lottie about your room yet… She…?

LOTTIE *enters.*

LOTTIE. Told me what about your room?

JESS. Nothing.

LOTTIE. What? Jess?… Poppy, what you talking about?

POPPY. Spill the beans.

JESS. Don't overreact… I've had to give up my therapy room.

LOTTIE. What?! Why?

JESS. I can't afford it right now.

LOTTIE. Why didn't you tell me?

JESS. What's the point? It's only until I get my car back!

LOTTIE. How come Poppy knows and I don't?

POPPY. I overheard her on the phone last week.

LOTTIE. I don't believe this…! Are things really that tight?… Have you told your parents?

JESS. I'm not fucking twelve!

LOTTIE *makes a face.*

Sorry… Look, I'm going through the appeals process. I'm waiting for my tribunal date. It's fine.

LOTTIE. Why do you always downplay things? It's not fine. It's outrageous!

POPPY. Jess doesn't do angry, remember?

LOTTIE. I'll lend you some money.

JESS. That's not the solution. Begging off my friends!

LOTTIE. Begging?! So what's happened to all your patients? Why aren't you more angry?

POPPY. Jess doesn't lose her rag. Dunno if she's even got a rag.

JESS. Look, they are not turning me into a victim.

LOTTIE. But you've worked so hard for this! I really think you should pick up the phone and call your folks. They'll help!

JESS *turns to* POPPY.

JESS. Poppy, do you need anything else before we go?

LOTTIE. I'm sick of this! (*Puts on her coat.*) You never tell me what's going on with you! (*To* POPPY.) She didn't even tell me she'd lost her car. Or that she'd broken up with Adam. I mean, what the fuck?! I've been your friend for twenty years. / Twenty years and you still shut me out!

JESS. Why are you so desperate to hear my problems?

LOTTIE. That's what friends do. I tell you all mine!

JESS. So?! That's your choice!

LOTTIE. You can't see how fucked up that is?

JESS. I just don't like talking about all this crap.

LOTTIE. Why?

JESS. It makes me feel…

LOTTIE. What?

JESS. Pathetic.

LOTTIE. Is that what you think of your patients? That they're pathetic?

JESS. You don't get it!

LOTTIE. Then tell me. I'm all ears. Come on... (*Waits*.) Fuck this. I'm going for a fag.

LOTTIE *leaves*.

POPPY. Well, that was kind of a row. A 'row-ette' maybe. You okay?

JESS. I just don't want to talk about this shit, okay?!

POPPY (*puts her hand on* JESS*'s face*). I hear you... Next week, we'll give that Hargreaves bloke hell at that public meeting.

JESS. I'm not going. Everyone's going to be angry, and shouting, and... I hate all that.

POPPY. We gotta go! We can't just let them get away with this.

JESS. You talk to him. That's more important.

POPPY. Why do you always fight for others but not yourself? Jess?

Beat.

JESS. Have you got your inhaler?

POPPY *holds it up to her*.

POPPY. You've got to come with us!

JESS *sits in silence on the bed*. POPPY *shuts her eyes*.

JESS *stands up to leave*. POPPY *grabs* JESS*'s hand*.

Jess... Don't go yet.

JESS *sits back down. Still holding* JESS*'s hand,* POPPY *drifts off to sleep*.

End of Act One.

ACT TWO

Scene One

*A community centre. Local constituents – a mix of disabled and
non-disabled people, including* JESS, LOTTIE, POPPY *and*
RITA *– are waiting for a meeting to commence.*

They sit facing a stage area where ANITA, *a smartly-dressed
and well-spoken woman, checks her phone while hovering by
a microphone in a stand.*

ANITA. Good evening, everyone. Oliver Hargreaves was held
up in traffic but he has just arrived. Thank you for your
patience. We're very pleased that he's squeezed this into his
hectic schedule…

   HENRY, *a scruffy-looking man in his late forties, intense
   and fragile, chips in.*

HENRY. He better not tell us to 'just be patient'!

   Laughter and jeers.

ANITA. Can I also, er, take this opportunity to thank you all
again for coming tonight. It's great to see so many new
faces here.

   HARGREAVES, *a well-groomed man in his sixties, enters
   the hall, flanked by a smartly dressed* FEMALE ADVISER.
   They head to the stage. A few people clap. The FEMALE
   ADVISER *stands at the side as* HARGREAVES *walks up to*
   ANITA. *After exchanging a few words, he takes off his coat
   and stands behind her as she speaks into the mic.*

   I know we're all pleased that our MP and DWP Minister,
   Oliver Hargreaves, is able to join us, so I'll now hand the
   floor over to him.

She sits down. A few people clap as HARGREAVES *steps towards the microphone. He speaks in a calm, self-assured manner.*

HARGREAVES. Thank you, Anita. Good evening. Apologies for my late arrival tonight. I appreciate you all waiting for me. Now, it has become apparent in my weekly surgeries that there's been some confusion and a degree of upset in the community about the changes to various benefits. And I thought that tonight would provide a good opportunity to address those concerns with as many of you as possible. So, without further ado, please raise your hand if you have a question.

Lots of hands go up, including POPPY*'s.*

The man up there. Raymond, isn't it?

RAYMOND *is stocky, middle-aged and rather aggressive at times. He stands up.*

RAYMOND. Yes! We met on election day. At Oldfield School.

HARGREAVES. I remember. How's your mother?

RAYMOND. She's ticking along. Thanks. So, where we live, there's a couple next door. They have three kids. I'm all for helping people who need it, but the dad, he's in his twenties. He used to work but now he's just at home. I got to say, he looks fighting fit to me.

HARGREAVES. Okay, well, there is a number you can call if you suspect benefit fraud.

RAYMOND. Yeah, I know. But I thought you should know too. All these people taking advantage. It's why you got my vote, Oliver.

HARGREAVES. Thank you, Raymond. I can't comment on your neighbour, but I feel very strongly about this issue too. It's just not fair, is it, on all the decent, hard-working people out there.

RAYMOND. I hear him playing in the garden with his kids. And his wife, she doesn't work either. She's from somewhere in Africa.

ANITA. So, who's next?   HARGREAVES. Okay, shall
                                        we...

HENRY. Are you talking about Mark Talbot? On Newhaven Road?

RAYMOND. Yes...?

HENRY. He's a mate of mine! He's got cancer.

RAYMOND. He doesn't look ill to me.

HENRY. You a doctor? He's on chemo!

Awkward silence. RAYMOND *and* HENRY *sit back down.*

HARGREAVES. I'm sorry to hear that. Henry, isn't it? I hope your friend makes a full recovery.

ANITA. Any more questions?

RAYMOND *looks annoyed. Hands go up.* POPPY *waves her hand around.*

HARGREAVES. The young gentleman in the blue shirt? What's your name?

RYAN, *a young man, stands up.*

RYAN. I'm Ryan.

HARGREAVES. Hello Ryan. Nice to meet you.

RYAN. I know there's been a lot of resistance to the new PIP benefit from the disabled community, but my sister was recently reassessed, and her benefit has actually gone up.

HARGREAVES. Yes, Ryan, the new criteria does help us target support to those with high care needs.

RYAN. My sister really appreciates the extra support.

HARGREAVES. Great. That's great.

HENRY. Why don't you two lovebirds get a room?

Laughter from the gathering.

Obviously a plant.

RYAN. I'm not a plant!

HENRY. That's what a plant would say!

More laughter.

HARGREAVES. Let's try and minimise the shouting out, please. And let's be civil. Who's next?

Hands shoot up, including POPPY*'s.* JESS *and* LOTTIE *point her out to* HARGREAVES.

LOTTIE. Over there!

HARGREAVES. The young lady in the... Over there?

POPPY. At last!

HARGREAVES. How can I help?

POPPY. Can you go toilet by yourself?

HARGREAVES. What's your name?

POPPY. Poppy.

HARGREAVES. Poppy. Hello. In answer to your question, yes, I am able to use the lavatory on my own.

POPPY. Lucky you! I can't. I need assistance. Recently, your lovely council cut –

HARGREAVES. Now, of course, the council doesn't make those –

POPPY. They cut all my night-time care. And I can't afford to go private, not now you keep finding me fit for work and cutting my ESA. This means two things. First, I am put to bed at nine o'clock every night. Do you know any twenty-one-year-olds who want to go to bed at nine? Now, I'm guessing you got up to all sorts of shenanigans when you were my age! And just cos I'm in this chair doesn't mean

I don't want to get up to that stuff too. This may shock you,
Mr H, but us crips, we get the horn just as much as you do!

Laughter and applause.

HARGREAVES. Thank you, I...

POPPY. Now, here's the rub. My night-time carers used to help
me get ready for bed when I wanted to go to bed. But now,
my last carer visits me at half-eight, and the next one comes
at half-seven in the morning. I have to be in bed by nine
now. That's ten-and-a-half hours when I can't get out of bed,
and I can't go to the loo. Do you know what I'm expected to
do? Wear a nappy!

Shocked noises.

I promise you, I do my best to hold it in. I drink and eat as
little as I can in the evenings. But sometimes, nature does its
thing. And out it comes. So, there I am, lying in my shit all
night. Sometimes it squidges out the sides and streaks over
the bed. I have a spray, citrus something. But the room just
smells of orangey poo instead. And in the morning, my carer,
Nads, she has to shower it off. It's not easy cos it's caked on
proper. So Nads, bless her, uses up most of her time cleaning
me up. Not to mention my bed. And that ain't how I thought
my days would start when I moved to your beautiful city.
I'm appealing the decision but –

HARGREAVES. Good for you –

POPPY. – here's my question. I know money's tight and all that,
but why can't I go to bed when I want to and why is you lot
making me sleep in my own piss and shit?

*Applause. A few people hold up phones to film what is
happening.*

HARGREAVES. Erm...

ANITA. Everyone! Could we ask people not to film the
meeting? Thank you.

She sits down. HARGREAVES *waits for people to stop but
some of them continue filming discreetly.*

HARGREAVES. I'd like to thank Poppy for her candour in sharing her story with us…

POPPY. Don't thank me. Just do something! I'm worried sick that my appeal will be rejected!

HARGREAVES. I'm sorry to hear about your experience, Poppy. There have clearly been some failings in the administration of care. I'd like to assure you that we are doing our best to address these teething problems. If you give my assistant, Anita, there, your details, I'll be happy to look into your case. When a government overhauls their welfare system, which we are in the midst of doing, there are always challenges, and mistakes are invariably made.

POPPY. My night hours weren't cut by mistake!

HARGREAVES. As I said, welfare reform presents many complex issues and we are trying to address them. But the system we are replacing was outdated and unwieldy. And, unfortunately, in the current global climate, difficult decisions have to be made.

HENRY. Difficult for who?

HARGREAVES. Difficult for government and society.

HENRY. But not the people sitting in their own shit?

HARGREAVES. This is about transferring to a better way of doing things. And saving the taxpayer money.

HENRY. You're happy to spend it when it suits you. You spend billions every year in fossil fuel subsidies, corporate tax breaks… You name it. Don't pretend this is about saving money!

HARGREAVES. With all due respect, Henry, I'm not pretending. We are trying to serve people's genuine needs while implementing a more cost-effective service.

POPPY. But you're not serving them!

HENRY. Exactly!

POPPY. And it's not just me. My friend here, her needs are being ignored too! Tell him, Jess.

LOTTIE *prods* JESS.

LOTTIE. Go on.

JESS. No!

LOTTIE. Go on!

JESS. Well, erm… I've just lost my Motability car and that means I can't get to work any more.

HARGREAVES. I'm sorry to hear that, Jess. Nobody wants that. These reforms are all about trying to help people to be more independent.

LOTTIE. But you've made her more dependent, not less!

HARGREAVES. That is certainly not the intention…

POPPY. I don't care what the intention was! Jess used to work and now she can't. Jess, tell him…

RAYMOND. We can't just give out cars to everyone!

JESS. No, let someone else speak!

ANITA. Thank you. I…

LOTTIE (*standing up*). She lost her car, then, as a result, she lost her job, and, now, has no income!

JESS *tugs at* LOTTIE*'s arm to try to stop her talking.*

POPPY. You're taking away the very support we need to be independent!

HARGREAVES. No, no, no. Listen. We are not removing support, we're updating the rules and criteria to better serve the people who need it.

LOTTIE. Then why are you reassessing people like Jess and Poppy every few years? They have lifelong conditions. / That's a fact, not an opinion!

HARGREAVES. The decision to reassess everybody is so we can make sure we can tailor support when changes occur, which they so often do.

RAYMOND. They're just trying to reduce disability benefit fraud!

HENRY. That was only half a per cent!

RAYMOND. That's not right! (*To* HARGREAVES.) Is it?

HARGREAVES. Anita?

ANITA. Er… Benefit fraud adds up to millions of pounds every year.

HENRY. But you're paying *billions* to private companies to do assessments that used to be done by doctors on the NHS!

LOTTIE. Yeah, how is that saving money?

HARGREAVES. You know, it was actually the other lot who brought in private companies to carry out assessments. But I agree that, handled properly, it's a system that will work more efficiently.

RAYMOND. Yeah! Get your facts right!

HENRY. How can a stranger be better placed to assess someone than their own GP? I've a friend with Asperger's and his assessor asked him, 'What's Asperger's?'! You couldn't make this shit up!

HARGREAVES. Look, we are aware that there have been some personnel issues and we are working hard to rectify them. These changes are about making the system function better for everybody.

LOTTIE. Well, they're making people's lives worse! Poppy and Jess are proof of that!

HARGREAVES. I'm sorry you feel this way. But, as we heard earlier from Ryan here, some people are finding this new system is providing better support.

RAYMOND. Yeah! You tell them, Ryan!

HENRY. Yeah, Ryan, earn your money!

Cheers and clapping.

ANITA. Any other questions?

KYLE, *a young man in a wheelchair, raises a hand. He has cerebral palsy and his speech is very unclear.*

KYLE. The council spent thousands of pounds adapting my bathroom and bedroom for me but I lost my flat a while ago because of the bedroom tax.

HARGREAVES. Erm, hello... your name is?

KYLE. Kyle.

HARGREAVES. Carl?

KYLE. Kyle!

HARGREAVES. Cal?

HENRY. Kyle!

HARGREAVES. Kyle. Sorry... I didn't catch what you said.

Beat.

HENRY. He said the council spent thousands of pounds adapting a flat for him but he lost it because of the bedroom tax.

HARGREAVES. Right. And where does he live now?

HENRY. What are you asking me for?!

HARGREAVES. Where do you live now, Kyle?

KYLE. I was moved to a third-floor attic flat with no lift. This is the first time I've been out in three months. My helper had to pull me down six flights of stairs. It took two hours.

HARGREAVES *has not understood a word.*

HENRY. He says he's been moved to a third-floor flat with no lift. And this is the first time he's been out in three months. His helper had to pull him down six flights of stairs. It took two hours.

Beat.

ANITA. I think we should –

HENRY. / Would you like me to repeat it?

HARGREAVES (*to* KYLE). I'm sorry to hear about your situation. It sounds, er…

KYLE. I was already stuck inside for eight months straight during lockdown! And I've had to stop my masters because I can't get to university.

HARGREAVES has not understood.

HENRY. He was already stuck inside for eight months straight during lockdown. He's had to give up his masters because he can't get to uni any more.

HARGREAVES. That is very unfortunate indeed. Really, this shouldn't be happening to my constituents. Er… If you give Anita, there, your details, I will see how we can help.

KYLE. Why the fuck would you help? You voted for the bedroom tax.

Applause. HARGREAVES *looks to* HENRY *for help.*

HENRY. He said he doesn't have much faith in the appeal process.

Laughter.

Listen. Austerity's never grown an economy. In hard times, you need to invest, not cut. But you know this. It's basic economics. Austerity's cost the UK over a hundred billion quid. This is about ideology, not economics.

RAYMOND. What do you know about economics?

HENRY. It's called reading. You should give it a crack.

Laughter. RAYMOND *looks humiliated.*

HARGREAVES. Covid has been a huge drain on public finances. We have risen to that challenge by spending around *four hundred billion* pounds on support packages so far. I'd call that pretty generous, wouldn't you? That's the equivalent of giving every person around five thousand pounds. Whatever your take on austerity, we have to tighten our belts where possible.

RAYMOND. Yep, that's right. We can't keep spending like there's no tomorrow!

ANITA. Okay, time for a few more questions.

RITA *puts up her hand.*

HARGREAVES. Yes, the lady in the jean jacket.

RITA *stands up. She's wearing a mask.*

RITA. I'm Rita... Erm... (*Reads from paper.*) I have OCD and agoraphobia. I was making good progress in therapy until my benefit was frozen after I missed an appointment at the Jobcentre. My doctor tried to explain to them that I'd had a... a bad day and couldn't leave my house but they... I've had to stop therapy... The system really discriminates against those with mental-health issues like agoraphobia.

RAYMOND. How come you made it out today if it's so bad?

As jeers ring out, RITA *sits down.*

HENRY. You should work for the Samaritans!

RAYMOND. Why don't you mind your own business? You're not even British.

HENRY. My mother is. I've been here since I was eighteen. And paid into the system ever since.

RAYMOND. Whatever. Why you even here? You're not disabled.

HENRY. I have a leg full of shrapnel and half my foot is missing. Car bomb when I served with your British army in Iraq. Remember the Iraq War? The illegal one all your papers told you to support? I'm deaf in this ear from the blast. My mate, Phil, wasn't so lucky. His head was blown off. Landed right on my lap. Ever seen a dismembered head, pal? Does things to you. Two years ago, I was diagnosed with PTSD, which I used to think was some middle-class bollocks like, what-do-ya-call-it?, 'chronic fatigue'. I finally went to therapy because my wife and kids couldn't cope with the screaming every night. Is that disabled enough for ya, Raymond?

RAYMOND *has no comeback so he sits down. Awkward silence.*

BOB *stands up. He is a black man in his late thirties.*

BOB. Firstly, I'm sorry to hear of your experiences, Henry. My dad died in combat... I'm Bob. I have a son, William. My wife and I both care for him. William is twenty and has profound learning and physical disabilities resulting from a rare illness he contracted at fifteen. He can't speak, eat, walk or hear. He receives PIP and ESA. For those who don't know, ESA is a benefit for those who can't work. Recently it was stopped, and we were told he'd been placed in a 'fit for work' group. Quite what job he is capable of doing remains a mystery.

KYLE. His job! (*Points to* HARGREAVES.)

BOB. We went through ten harrowing months appealing that decision. And we won, but my amazing wife, Marcella, had a stroke last year. I lost my business. Covid. Got nothing.

MARCELLA. I feel so guilty. Now I'm in this – (*Points to wheelchair.*) poor Bob has to look after both of us.

BOB. Don't say that, honey. You said you wouldn't.

HARGREAVES. Alright, I think we should...

BOB. We love Will to bits. But it's not easy caring for him. With all the care and support in the world, it wouldn't be easy. Our bathroom isn't accessible so, for five years, we've had to wash him in a paddling pool in our lounge. It shouldn't be so hard to get the right support.

MARCELLA. It's so hard. But when he laughs and looks at you with those dark cheeky eyes...

BOB. You and your party make us fight so hard for every bit of help. Our family have to prove ourselves over and over again. As if we're criminals. You spoke about being civil earlier but how can we be a civilised society when those with real and complex needs are being punished for having them?

Cheering and clapping. ANITA *and the* FEMALE ADVISER *look nervous.*

HARGREAVES. Bob, I am sorry things have been so difficult.
And I will do my best to help you get more support. I will –

BOB. / Gimme a date then! Come on!

HARGREAVES. Look, I am confident that things will improve,
but Covid has meant that we are dealing with huge…

KYLE. Sixty per cent of English Covid deaths in 2020 were
disabled people!

HARGREAVES. Sixty… (*Struggling to piece together* KYLE's
words.) per cent… of English Covid…

HENRY.…deaths in 2020 were disabled people.

HARGREAVES. Covid has exposed some real inequalities that
we are keen to address. But I would ask you all to bear with
us while the country gets back on its feet, and just be patient.

HENRY. Bingo! He said it!!

Laughter. HARGREAVES *is baffled.*

Our patience is running out. I don't believe your words.
You know exactly how many people are suffering because of
your cuts, but still, you keep cut, cut, cutting like a fuckin'
hairdresser on crack. Don't keep using Covid as an excuse!
It was exactly the same before Covid, before Brexit. People,
planet? Trash 'em both! This system isn't 'failing' or 'under
pressure'. It's working *exactly* how it's designed to work.
Cos your goal is to create a society where there is no
compassion, no support network, no social responsibility.
Basically, America! You don't want people having any
expectations of help if they get sick or injured. Cos if you
don't help people like us, you don't have to help anyone!

Cheering. HARGREAVES's *phone rings and he silences it.*

HARGREAVES. I'm afraid I really don't share your very
cynical conclusions. I assure you that we want to improve
things. We want a system that works efficiently. That's why
we're putting better rules in place in order to discourage
unhealthy welfare dependency. We very much believe that
most people, with the right support, can be part of the
workforce. Disabled or not.

KYLE. What do you know about being disabled or sick?

HARGREAVES. Erm…

POPPY. He said, what do you know about being disabled or sick?

HARGREAVES. I don't have extensive knowledge, which is why I am trying very hard to listen and learn from my constituents. It's why I'm here today, believe it or not.

KYLE. Have you ever been incapacitated in any way?

HARGREAVES. Incap…? Incapac…?

LOTTIE. Have you ever been incapacitated in any way?

HARGREAVES. I have, actually. I had a bad accident when I was sixteen. I broke my leg and couldn't walk.

KYLE. How long for?

HARGREAVES. How long for? Well, I fractured my leg badly in two places. I was lying in my hospital bed feeling sorry for myself. The doctor came by and told me that I wouldn't walk for four months…

POPPY. Get the violins out!

HARGREAVES. …My father leaned over and whispered, 'Prove him wrong. Walk in three!' And I did. I was brought up to believe that a positive, can-do attitude goes a long way.

Beat.

JESS. Did you fall off a horse?

HARGREAVES. Sorry?

JESS. Did you fall off a horse?

HARGREAVES *stares at her in astonishment.*

Scene Two

Rehab centre. A small room.

JESS *sits in a chair. She waits.* AIDAN *enters.*

AIDAN. Why are you here? I'm not your patient any more.

JESS. And I'm not your therapist.

AIDAN. So, what do we call ourselves now?

JESS. Aidan and Jess? How are you?

AIDAN. Off the booze. Since my birthday blip. They're talking about letting me out for 'good behaviour'. I'll ask again. Why are you here?

JESS. I met your dad.

> AIDAN *stares at her.*

AIDAN. Lucky you.

JESS. Why didn't you tell me who he was?

AIDAN. Where did you meet him?

JESS. At a public meeting. He told the story about falling off the horse.

AIDAN. Nice guy, huh?... So, does this make it easier to understand why I'm so fucked up?

JESS. I don't think you're fucked up.

AIDAN. I wouldn't be here if I wasn't.

JESS. You're in pain. That's different. I have a lot of respect for you.

> AIDAN *sits down.*

AIDAN (*scornfully*). Why? Because I had it so hard being his son?

JESS. No. Because you're not like him.

AIDAN. What am I like then?

JESS. Different.

Beat.

AIDAN. 'Different'… He took me hunting once. Hated it. He told me to stop being 'soft'.

JESS. Why do you think he sees empathy as weakness?

AIDAN. Because he's an arsehole.

JESS. But people don't create themselves. We're all shaped by biology… environment.

AIDAN. And that's it. We can't change?

JESS. We can try. But it's hard. As you know.

AIDAN. Wow, I never thought you'd be making excuses for him. Especially now you've met him.

JESS. I'm just saying, there are reasons why people are the way they are.

AIDAN. Should we all feel sorry for him, then? Poor little Oliver.

JESS. Do you think he's happy?

AIDAN. I think he's powerful.

JESS. That isn't the same thing.

AIDAN. I don't know. And I don't care.

JESS. Do you know much about his childhood?

AIDAN. No. And if I tell you what I do know, you'll probably feel sorry for him, and I don't think I could handle that. Actually, I think it would make me put my fist through a fucking wall… His mum died in childbirth.

JESS. Did you know his father?

AIDAN. No.

JESS. What happened after his mum died?… Aidan.

AIDAN. Erm… (*Sighs.*) His Aunt Lily moved in. Then he was sent to boarding school, I think.

JESS. At what age?

AIDAN. Six.

JESS. God, that's young.

AIDAN. Well, he says he's glad he went.

JESS. How many six-year-olds want to be sent to boarding school?

AIDAN. Don't try and make me feel fucking bad for him!

He leaps out of his chair. JESS *recoils in shock.*

I can't do this.

JESS. Why does it make you so angry?

AIDAN. Because… You know, for someone who isn't my therapist, this feels alarmingly like therapy.

JESS. We're just talking. But I can go.

AIDAN. No, let's turn the spotlight on you now. Have you ever felt like you're not good enough?

JESS. Yes.

AIDAN. Because of your parents?

JESS. No.

AIDAN. Why then?… See, you don't like the deep, probing questions either, do you?

AIDAN *sits down.*

I didn't think so. (*Gets back up.*) Thanks for dropping by. (*Walks away.*)

JESS. I didn't feel good enough because… I was born into a world that told me I wasn't.

AIDAN *stops.*

A world that labelled me as broken, brain-damaged, faulty. Ugly words that made me feel ugly. I never saw anyone like me in books or films. Doctors told me to do exercises so I would walk and talk the 'right' way. Because I did them the 'wrong' way. So, what did I do? I stopped going out. Shut myself in my room with my books for about a year. I was twenty and I hated myself. Then, one morning, I sat up, and there was a patch of sunlight on my bed. Where my feet were. And, for some reason, I thought, wow, I'm alive because of my body. This shaky body I had resented for so long. And, here it was, giving me my life. I felt my heart, loyally beating away. Suddenly, I felt this surge of gratitude for this beautiful, messy life in my wobbly body. I laughed out loud. Then I apologised to my arms and legs for being so ungrateful. I felt defiant, like… I'm not broken. I'm a unique spark of life. We all are! That joy in my stomach never went. But I still don't really like my voice. It's not how it sounds in my head.

AIDAN. What does it sound like to you?

JESS. A Radio Four announcer! Anyway, I don't want to let those fuckers rob me of a single day more.

AIDAN. What fuckers are they, then?

JESS. The fuckers who make us believe there's a 'right' way to be… There is no objective normal, or beautiful or successful. They're just made up to disempower us.

AIDAN. What, you think there's some big master plan to keep us all fragmented and unhappy?

JESS. I think liking yourself is a political act.

AIDAN. You should do a TED Talk.

JESS. I should get going.

AIDAN. Hypothetically, if I wanted to start our sessions again, would that be possible? If I did.

JESS. Yes. Oh, but… I've had to give up my room for a bit. We could do them here?

AIDAN. No.

JESS. How about Zoom?

AIDAN. How about your place?

JESS. I only have a small flat.

AIDAN. Is there room for a recovering pisshead and two chairs?

Beat.

JESS. Erm… That's not allowed. Let me know if you change your mind about here.

AIDAN. I won't.

He walks out.

Scene Three

POPPY*'s studio flat.*

JESS *and* LOTTIE *are with* POPPY*, who is very upset. She and* LOTTIE *drink from bottles of beer.*

LOTTIE. We'll appeal again. We will!

POPPY. How's that gonna help? They've just rejected this one. And on the phone, they hinted that I might have to go into a care home if I'm not… (*Mimics official voice.*) 'happy with my level of support'! No, I'm not 'happy', you fuckers! I'm raging!

JESS. But I'll help you this time!

POPPY *lets out a big sigh and drinks more beer.*

POPPY. Even if we do win, how long's that gonna take? I'm not rotting away in bed for God knows how long! And I'm not gonna be dumped in a stale-piss-stinking care home. No way!

LOTTIE *rubs* POPPY*'s shoulders.*

That hurts, sorry.

LOTTIE *stops.*

LOTTIE. Pops, we won't let you be dumped anywhere. Jess is right. You have to keep optimistic.

POPPY (*bitterly*). Why? They don't give a shit about me! You saw Hargreaves. He had an answer for everything! Seriously, how do these fuckers end up in power?

JESS. And the people you'd actually trust with power don't want it.

POPPY. Er, newsflash. That's never going to change!

JESS. It might. We just need a new rule… Anyone who wants power, can't have it!

POPPY. It's the selfish wankers who fight hardest for it. So we're all fucked. Life is unfair. The end.

LOTTIE. Pops, don't give up hope.

POPPY. Why? I still have to go to bed in a nappy!… Get me another beer, will you? I want to get shitfaced. I shouldn't drink more so late in the day, but fuck it…

LOTTIE *brings* POPPY *a beer and she takes a big gulp.*

LOTTIE. I keep thinking of that guy, Raymond, at the meeting. He was so… heartless to everyone.

POPPY. Yeah, but that PTSD bloke took him down big time.

JESS. Oh, I think he just humiliated him. He probably went home feeling even more angry.

POPPY. Jess – the world's expert on being angry. By the way, did you hear all those stories at the meeting? Still convinced your benefit was 'cut by mistake'?

LOTTIE. Shall we have a joint?

POPPY. None left. Skint… In other cheerful news, Baz's been thrown out of the care home. He hired an escort. And the rules say randy disabled lads can't fuck when they want to.

JESS. Where is he now?

POPPY. Back home. To his doormat mum and abusive stepdad. I mean, grown men are allowed to pay for sex! It's so screwed up.

LOTTIE. Yeah, but…

POPPY downs some more beer. JESS and LOTTIE look on with concern.

POPPY. I had a mate back home… Zara. Worked as an escort. Had some disabled punters. She said she felt she was doing a good thing. I was like, damn right, you are! We all need to be touched and stroked and fucked. Whatever body we have. How is that not obvious?!

LOTTIE. I get what you're saying, but I'm not a fan of women being prostitutes.

POPPY. That's for them to decide! Feminism isn't about telling other women what to do! If a woman wants to help a disabled man have a sex life, that's a good thing in my book! Some guys can't even wank. Imagine not being able to wank when you want to? *(Drinks.)* I'd pay for sex if I needed to. Totally.

Beat.

I can't believe I voted for Hargreaves's lot.

JESS. What? Are you joking?

LOTTIE. Jess!

POPPY. No. I voted for them.

JESS. Why?!

POPPY. My grandparents always did. Said the other lot would turn us into Russia.

JESS. The other lot wanted to put an end to all this shit!

POPPY. Wake up, Jess. They're all the same. A bunch of power-hungry tossers. You said so yourself!

JESS. Did you actually read the manifestos?

LOTTIE. Don't –

POPPY. Oh, yeah… No! Who does that?!

JESS. Then how do you know what you're voting for?

POPPY. I ain't got time to read that bullshit!

JESS. And that's why we're in this mess…

POPPY. What, cos people like me are too thick? Is that it, Jess? Cos I have a TV and don't like reading fucking books like you? Spit it out! I know you don't swallow.

LOTTIE. Come on, we're all on the same side here!

JESS. I can't believe you voted for this. And it doesn't just affect you. We're all affected… Do you not get that?

LOTTIE. Jess!

POPPY. Finally, it's Angry Jess! Hello.

JESS. Is that all you can say?

POPPY. So I've got it all wrong, have I? Are you also gonna tell me that immigrants aren't overloading the NHS, and the country ain't broke?

JESS. What? Immigrants pay more in taxes / than they take…

POPPY. More woke bullshit!

LOTTIE. Can we just all calm down? We need to stay strong and together.

POPPY. Who are you? You ain't even strong enough to come out to your old man!

LOTTIE. What? Fuck you!

LOTTIE *looks upset. The three women sit in silence.*

POPPY. I'm not stupid, you know.

JESS. I never said that. Or thought it.

POPPY. The way you talk… it's like you're right and everyone else is wrong.

JESS. I just hate hearing you trot out their lies.

POPPY. There you go again! Making out I'm some kind of brainwashed moron!

JESS. I'm not! I just think… We all need to look at the facts out there.

POPPY (*angry*). This country's in massive debt. Fact –

JESS. Yes, but –

POPPY. Covid's made that worse. We have to make cuts. Fact –

JESS. Covid didn't make –

POPPY. You should piss off now. Fact!

> JESS *stares at her.*

> Bravo for staying controlled! Go on, call me a stupid, little cunt… Just shout back at me like a real fucking person! Oh, I forgot, Jess can't bear to make a fuss about anything cos she can't be a mere mortal like the rest of us!

> JESS *starts to leave.*

> Okay, go and get on your high horse where you belong. Shoot me for not being as perfect as you… You middle-class lefties are so fucking judgemental. No wonder you always lose.

JESS. This isn't about left or right! This is about how we treat each other. That's what politics is!… Poppy, what hope have we got if *we're* voting for Hargreaves?!

POPPY. Fuck you and fuck hope.

> *She raises her bottle to* JESS *then takes another swig.*

Scene Four

JESS's living room/kitchen. JESS is at the table, on the phone. A bowl of pasta sits in front of her, untouched. There is a letter beside it.

JESS. Yes… I just got the letter… But my tribunal date is eight months away. I can't survive till then with no car!… Yes, I know it's not your fault… Okay, bye.

She hangs up and makes another call. We hear Poppy's voice.

POPPY (*voice-over*). It's Poppy. I'm probably tied up with a hot guy right now – literally, ha! Leave a message.

JESS ends the call and makes another one.

JESS. Hi, I've got a question about how to appeal against night-care hours being cut… It's for a friend… Okay.

Tinny music is played. JESS waits. Every now and then, the music stops and we hear:

VOICE-OVER. Thank you for calling the Citizens Advice Bureau. All our advisers are busy right now…

She waits and waits. The tinny music gets louder and louder until it's deafening.

AIDAN enters, carrying a bag.

AIDAN. Hi…

JESS. Hi.

JESS hangs up. AIDAN looks around.

AIDAN. Thanks for agreeing to see me.

He puts down his bag and sits down.

JESS. You know this isn't therapy?

AIDAN. That's against the rules.

JESS. Yes.

AIDAN. I am totally clear this is a non-therapy session. We're just Aidan and Jess.

JESS. What did you want to tell me?

AIDAN. I wrote to Dad's aunt, Lily. You remember I mentioned her? She wrote back... I wanted to tell you what she said.

JESS. About what?

AIDAN. Dad.

He takes out a handwritten letter and unfolds it.

Can I read you this bit... That okay?

JESS *nods.* AIDAN *reads from the letter.*

'Ever since he was little, your father's dream was to be an artist. I was never very good with children but I could see how much he loved painting. He would paint whenever he could, for hours on end. He always had a smudge on his cheek or forehead. One Christmas, he must have been about thirteen, he painted his first self-portrait. He set himself up with an old mirror in the playroom and painted for hours on end. I tried to take a peek but he wouldn't let me. When he finally finished, he came into the kitchen where Richard' – (*Looks at* JESS.) that's his father – (*Reading.*) 'and I were having tea. He gave the painting to him. Oli was beaming. It was the best painting he'd ever done. Just beautiful. Richard looked at him and said, "No son of mine is going to be a painter." He tore the painting in half. Oli started to cry. Richard just said "Don't be soft", and walked out. He never did understand his son. Oli was always a sensitive boy. That night, he begged me to help, to talk to Richard for him. But I didn't know how to. I couldn't. That was the last time Oli painted. Something went out in him that day.

AIDAN *folds up the letter, pockets it, then reaches into his bag and takes out the two halves of young Hargreaves's self-portrait. He holds them up in front of* JESS.

She kept it.

JESS. Wow.

They stare at the painting.

He looks so… sweet.

AIDAN. Oli…

AIDAN *puts the painting on the table.*

That pasta looks rancid.

JESS. It is.

AIDAN. Want me to cook you something else? I'm not brilliant but I'm pretty sure I can beat rancid.

JESS. No. Thanks.

AIDAN *walks over to the sofa.*

AIDAN. Can I lie down on this?

JESS. Yes.

AIDAN *lies on the sofa and stares at the ceiling.*

AIDAN. I didn't know he wasn't allowed to… be himself either. But I had a Maeve. He didn't… I've never seen him cry. Not even at Mum's funeral… She was the love of his life. I just can't get my head around it… That he used to be like that…

JESS. We all start out that way. Beautiful, innocent, fragile.

AIDAN. I still don't know if I can ever forgive him.

JESS. You need to try. Not for him. For you.

AIDAN *mulls this over. He sits up and looks at* JESS.

AIDAN. Could you?

JESS. I hate what he's doing.

AIDAN. But?

JESS. I think he learnt, early on, that life is harsh… you knuckle down, feelings don't matter.

AIDAN. So it's not his fault he's a bad person? Isn't it patronising? That he's just been shaped by his past?

JESS. We all are. And we don't choose how we grow up, how we see the world... ourselves. That's why I don't think it's about being 'good' or 'bad'. But I do think he should be kept away from power. Hurt people hurt people.

They sit in silence.

AIDAN. Fucked-up systems need fucked-up people. That's why you're a therapist, right?

JESS. That. Plus my yacht.

Beat.

AIDAN. I know so many good people who vote for my dad.

JESS. Me too.

Beat.

AIDAN. I've never thought of my dad as a victim. I just saw him as this cold... cut-off person.

JESS. Yeah, but you don't cut off unless you're hurt.

AIDAN. Jess... I wanted to say...

NADIA *bursts in. She stands there, frozen.*

JESS. What's wrong? Nads?

NADIA. She... Poppy...

NADIA *can say no more.*

The lighting changes to show time passing.

LOTTIE *runs in.*

I was late... As always... I... I kept calling her, on the phone, to tell her, but there was no answer. I opened the door and the smell... She'd cut her wrists. She was just lying there in bed, staring at me. She looked so small... Moja mala Poppy.

NADIA *starts to cry.* AIDAN *hands her a tissue.*

LOTTIE. What did the police say?

NADIA. Not much. They took her away. In black bag. It was too big for her.

They sit in silence.

I feel like it's my fault.

JESS. Don't say that!

LOTTIE. Nadia…

NADIA. She kept saying they'd force her into a care home. I kept saying, no, that wouldn't happen. I wouldn't let that happen!

JESS. We had a row…

LOTTIE. Yeah.

NADIA. Did you think she would ever…?

JESS. Never… No.

NADIA. She was so small. But there was so much blood. The sheets were red. (*Upset.*) Sorry!

LOTTIE. Nadia, don't say sorry.

NADIA *sits down on the sofa.* JESS *shuffles over and takes her hand.*

NADIA. Last night, as I was leaving, I turned back to check on her… I don't know why… and she was lying there… staring at the ceiling. I went home and I prayed.

LOTTIE. Why?

NADIA. I thought she was dulling… darkening. I felt it here. (*Pats her heart.*) Like a pain. Yesterday, she didn't want to talk much, so I let her be. We all feel like that sometimes. I told her I might be late today because I had to buy her some food. She said she was low on money but I said I'd buy her a few things myself. She said she wasn't hungry. She's said that a lot, lately… I helped her to the loo, she did her teeth… the normal stuff we do. She was quiet. But she asked how you were. She told me to say hi… And as I was leaving, she said, 'Ta, Nads, for everything.'

NADIA's phone rings. She composes herself and answers.

NADIA. Hello?… Can you hang on? (*To* JESS.) It's the police.

She gets up and leaves.

LOTTIE. She told that cunt Hargreaves how desperate she was… and he just fobbed her off!

AIDAN. Er, I've got to… Sorry… (*Rushes out.*)

LOTTIE. What's his problem?

JESS shrugs. She looks upset.

Are you okay?

Long beat.

JESS shuffles over to the exercise bike and starts cycling angrily.

LOTTIE follows and sits on the floor in front of her. JESS cycles away, staring straight ahead.

Say something. Please.

JESS. There is no room for us.

LOTTIE. What do you mean?

JESS. Me. Poppy. Baz… In this culture. We don't fit anywhere. We're no use to anyone.

LOTTIE. Don't say that.

JESS. It's true. To deal with difference you need empathy and… imagination. But they're just stamped on in this world… We're not human beings with hearts and minds and dreams, we're just cogs in a giant, fucking… unhappiness machine. Work till you die! And if you can't be a cog, they'll kill you. The end.

LOTTIE. Jess, do not let them make you feel / like that…

JESS. You know, when I was born, the doctor told my parents I'd never lead a normal life. When I heard that, I thought,

'Who wants a normal life? I want a fucking amazing life!'
I was so lucky my parents chose to reject that crap and just...
loved me. Poppy didn't have any of that. And now...

Beat.

LOTTIE *takes out her phone and plays Nirvana's 'Lithium'.*

JESS *stops cycling, panting heavily as the music fills the
space.*

POPPY *zooms across the stage in her wheelchair, smoking
a joint.*

Scene Five

HARGREAVES*'s constituency office.* JESS *is sitting in the
empty waiting area.* ANITA *enters.*

ANITA. Hello... Can I help you?

JESS. I'd like to see Oliver Hargreaves.

ANITA. Do you have an appointment?

JESS. No.

ANITA. Let me check the diary. (*Pops to her desk.*) Ah, things
are a bit manic for the next few weeks... He's got a
documentary crew following him around, so he's extra-busy.

JESS. I need to see him today. About my friend.

ANITA. He won't be able to see you, I'm afraid.

JESS. I'll wait. Just in case.

RAYMOND *enters. He walks over to* ANITA.

RAYMOND. Ta, Anita. Can I take a few leaflets? I'll pop them
through a few doors on my way home.

ANITA (*gives* RAYMOND *some leaflets*). You're a real trooper, thanks.

ANITA*'s phone beeps. She reads a text.*

Excuse me... Oliver needs me.

RAYMOND. Of course.

ANITA *exits.*

RAYMOND *turns to leave. He spots* JESS *for the first time and stops. He moves towards her and sits down in the chair next to her.*

You're that girl from the meeting... Oi, I'm talking to you!

He prods her arm.

JESS. What?

RAYMOND. You were there at the meeting. At the community centre, remember? Why are you here?

JESS *turns away.*

Don't ignore me.

JESS. What do you want?

RAYMOND. My dad was a copper. Got shot in the knee. Could barely walk. Did he moan? Did he go on benefits? No. He worked till he dropped dead. Now, it's just me and Mum. She's got Parkinson's. I work seven nights a week to look after her. I've got a heart condition. And you know what? We've never asked for a handout. Not like you and your friends. Bleeding the country dry... Gone all quiet now, haven't we?!

JESS. Have you finished?

RAYMOND (*riled*). You'll know when I've finished. I'm not a bad person. I pay my taxes. I help old people. I get up on the Tube when I see a pregnant woman. You know what gets me about people like you? You think the world owes you something. It doesn't.

JESS. What's so bad about helping each other?

RAYMOND (*menacingly*). Your lot can't help anybody. Just take, take, take. Scrounger!

JESS thinks RAYMOND is going to strike her, and her arms fly up to protect her face.

(*Shocked.*) I'm not going to hit you. I'm not going to hit you! Who do you think I am?

JESS lowers her arms.

RAYMOND stares at her, still shocked. Voices are heard. RAYMOND walks out.

ANITA enters.

ANITA. I'm afraid Oliver's just started a conference call so he won't be able to see you today.

She leaves. JESS sits alone.

Scene Six

JESS's living room/kitchen. ANGELA, a tired-looking carer in her fifties, walks in carrying a blouse for JESS.

ANGELA. I could only find this.

JESS. Wasn't there a T-shirt in the top drawer?

ANGELA. Oh I thought you said the third drawer. Can you wear this?

JESS. Okay.

JESS takes off her top.

ANGELA. Can you put it on?

JESS. Can you help me?

ANGELA. How exactly?

JESS. Can you help me put it on and do up the buttons?

ANGELA *puts the blouse on* JESS.

ANGELA. Why do they make the buttons so fiddly?

ANGELA*'s phone beeps several times.*

That'll be my son. I'm in a rush. (*Buttons up the top.*) Sorry. Anything else?

JESS. No. Thanks.

ANGELA (*checks her phone*). The WiFi's really bad in here.

JESS. Is it?

ANGELA. Can I go?

JESS. Yes.

ANGELA. Bye.

JESS. Bye.

ANGELA *walks out.*

JESS *takes out her phone, considers making a call but changes her mind. Moments later, the lights go off. Darkness.*

Shit!

JESS *drops to the floor and waits. But the lights don't come back on.*

She takes out her phone and dials. A recording of an old lady's voice speaking in Spanish:

VOICE-OVER. Hola, deja un mensaje para Gloria.

The answer-machine beeps.

JESS (*on the phone*). Hi, Mum and Dad... I...

She hangs up, bangs the phone on the floor and throws the phone away.

(*Screaming.*) Fuuuuuuck!

Silence.

AIDAN (*offstage*). Jess?

AIDAN enters.

Hi. Why you sitting in the dark?

JESS. Power cut.

AIDAN. The street lamps are on.

JESS doesn't answer.

Have you got any candles? Hang on. (*Turns on the torch on his phone.*) Okay. Where are they?

JESS. By the mirror in the hall.

AIDAN finds the candles. He returns and lights them with a lighter.

Thanks. You smoke?

AIDAN. Used to. I still keep it on me. Habit, I guess.

AIDAN sits on the floor.

I brought you this…

He takes out an orange and rolls it to JESS.

I wanted to drop by sooner, but… I thought you might not want to see me.

JESS. I called the centre.

AIDAN. Yeah? They let me out. I'm back home…

JESS. Great.

Beat.

AIDAN. It was pretty shocking. What happened with Poppy.

Beat.

I'm really sorry. About my dad… About everything.

JESS smiles sadly.

How is Nadia doing?

JESS. Not good. Off work. Doctor's orders.

AIDAN. And Lottie?

JESS. Caring for her mum. She's dying, poor thing... I was
worried. When you ran off.

AIDAN. I tried so hard to push you away, Jess. And here I am.
Bruised but sober. I wanted... I needed to say thank you.

Beat.

How are you?

JESS. Fine.

AIDAN. Really?

JESS. Okay, you heard me scream my head off, didn't you?

AIDAN. Want to talk about it?

JESS. No.

AIDAN. I bet when your patients say that, you tell them it
probably means they should talk about it.

JESS. Aidan, I appreciate you coming round. But I'm not going
to share my shit with you.

AIDAN. Why not?

JESS. Because it's mine. Not yours.

AIDAN. You helped me with mine. Why don't you do what you
tell your patients to do?

JESS. Because I'm an intransigent fucker.

AIDAN. Who do *you* lean on?... Jess?

JESS. My family... Lottie. If I have to.

AIDAN. Is anyone else allowed in that tiny circle?... (*Clicks
his fingers.*) We could talk about the Tube first if you like.
Or the weather. While I stroke my beard and look pensive.

JESS. Aidan...

AIDAN. Humour me… Just let it out. Say something. Anything.

Beat.

JESS. I… Poppy… She always said I was so 'controlled'…
I think it's maybe because I lack control over my body, so,
you know, I try to control other stuff.

Beat.

When you're wobbly… you have to ask for help. All the
time. 'Can you pour me a drink?' 'Can you cut up my food?'
'Can you undo my buttons?' You're always asking for help!

AIDAN. You feel your 'asking for help' quota is full?

JESS. Yeah. I do.

AIDAN. But helping people is the best part of life. You know
that, Jess… Let others help you.

JESS. You know, whenever I see myself in the mirror or on
video, I'm always shocked by how shaky I look. How
vulnerable I am. I want to be strong.

AIDAN. Bottling everything up isn't being strong. You have to
let people in. Wobbly or not.

JESS. Anyway, my life is a mess right now. And I thought you
were scared of messy.

AIDAN. I was. But I met this really good therapist, well, non-
therapist, actually. She taught me that messy is part of living
and feeling and loving. And that wobbly was rock-solid.

JESS. Did she?

AIDAN. She did.

JESS. She sounds quite good.

AIDAN. She is. But she needs to lean on other people sometimes.

JESS. Maybe she's scared to lean on them, to be even more
vulnerable.

AIDAN. Maybe she needs to realise that leaning on people isn't
being weak. We all do it.

JESS. When I was at school, my careers adviser told me I was good with people so I should work in a shop. I said I wanted to be a therapist. She said she didn't think I was cut out for that... I tried so hard to prove her wrong. I went to uni, I studied hard. I got my PhD. I became a therapist. I did it. I loved my work. It showed the world my value, loud and clear. I felt useful. And now I've lost it and I just don't know who I am without it. Well, I do. I'm a wobbly girl with no work and no life.

AIDAN. Don't say that.

JESS. It's true. I thought love and kindness and empathy were the answers to everything... You know, this man called me a scrounger the other day, and there was a part of me, I hate saying this, that felt he was right. That joy in me, that I told you about, it's gone...

AIDAN. And your electricity's been cut off too...

Beat.

Jess, you're a fighter... And you don't have to keep proving yourself to the world! You're enough.

JESS. That's not what the voice in my head says.

AIDAN. The Radio Four announcer? She can do one.

Beat.

JESS. I hate this fighting.

AIDAN. You can't let them win, Jess. You said I mentioned rules a lot. And I did. My dad loves rules. (*Imitates his dad.*) 'Strict parent to the unruly masses.' But it's all bollocks!

JESS. But he's made me feel like... I don't belong any more.

AIDAN. You don't belong. Not in his world. With your wobbles and giant heart and huge swirling imagination. You're never going to belong. Thank God you don't. He was crushed and his world is full of... self-loathing and pain and fear. And a million fucking rules! It's crushing everything valuable around us right now. He wants to force you into the world that he was forced into. But you won't ever fit. Because all the things you embody – love, empathy, creativity – they belong in a world which is shaped by hope. A beautiful world. You belong there. All of us do, really, Jess.

Beat.

JESS. *You* should do a TED Talk.

AIDAN. Keep fighting for that world. We need it more than ever.

Beat.

JESS. But I'm a fucking mess right now. Look at me!

AIDAN. Yes, but you're the most beautiful mess I've ever seen.

JESS *smiles*.

Don't.

JESS. What?

AIDAN. Smile.

JESS. Why?

AIDAN. Because when you smile, I forget to breathe.

AIDAN *leans into* JESS *and kisses her. She pulls away, her eyes fixed on his.*

We're just Aidan and Jess, remember?

JESS. We can't do this. It's not…

AIDAN (*holds a finger to* JESS*'s lips*).
I do not ask for anything.
Just that you know
my love for you fills the skies,
and drowns the moon.
And till I fade one day soon,
I will thank the cosmos
and the clusters of stardust too
for gently colliding
and forging you.

JESS. Please tell me you wrote that.

AIDAN *nods.*

JESS *gives in to the moment. They kiss deeply and embrace.*
JESS *pulls* AIDAN*'s top off. They kiss.* JESS *pulls away*
suddenly.

Aidan…

AIDAN. What?

JESS. Can you undo my buttons?

AIDAN *undoes her buttons and they kiss.*

Scene Seven

HARGREAVES*'s constituency office. A camera and filming*
equipment are set up. HARGREAVES *and* ANITA *walk in.*

HARGREAVES. Did you find out who else is on the panel
tomorrow?

ANITA. Barry's doing it.

HARGREAVES *pulls a face.*

HARGREAVES. They obviously want a rematch of last time.
Car-crash number two.

ANITA. That won't happen. We have answers for every
possible line of attack. We have…

HARGREAVES. 'We'? Who's doing the show? Me or you?

ANITA. Sorry, I just meant…

HARGREAVES. I'll be the one taking the flak if it goes tits-up
again. It won't be 'we' then.

A CAMERAPERSON *and* SOUND-WOMAN *enter.*
The CAMERAPERSON *holds the camera up to film*
HARGREAVES. ANITA *adjusts* HARGREAVES*'s tie.*

ANITA. Okay, great. Shall we pick up from where we left off and then call it a day?

The CAMERAPERSON *puts their thumb up and signals to* HARGREAVES *to start.*

HARGREAVES. So, I won't lie, welfare has been a complex area to navigate. But I believe that we must all step up when challenging situations come along. We can't always expect life to unfold the way we'd like it to and we need to face whatever the future holds, head-on. That's how we make progress, collectively. Indeed, one of my guiding beliefs is that politicians should empower people by breaking this chronic dependency culture and by encouraging responsibility. It's important that we…

Suddenly, HARGREAVES *is interrupted by* BOB *walking in pushing his wife,* MARCELLA, *in a wheelchair. Then* RITA *enters and* KYLE *in his electric wheelchair, followed by* HENRY, *who looks tired and dirty, and walks with a crutch.* JESS *and* AIDAN *come in last.*

ANITA. Erm… We're in the middle of filming here. You can't just barge in like this!

HARGREAVES *sees* AIDAN *and stops in his tracks.*

HARGREAVES (*shocked*). Aidan?! What are you…

AIDAN. Hi, Dad.

HARGREAVES. What are you doing here?

Beat.

HARGREAVES *regains his composure.*

ANITA. Let's stop the filming.

HARGREAVES. No, I've got nothing to hide.

ANITA. Okay…

HARGREAVES (*to* JESS). Why have you dragged my son here?

AIDAN. It was my idea.

HARGREAVES. What?

AIDAN. Human rights aren't won by obedient folk, Dad.

ANITA. I will call the police if you don't leave now.

AIDAN. We're not leaving.

HARGREAVES. Why are you here?

JESS. Do you remember Poppy?

HARGREAVES. Poppy... Poppy who?

JESS. The girl in the wheelchair who spoke at your public
    meeting.

HARGREAVES. Ah... yes.

JESS. She killed herself. Two weeks after that.

    Awkward silence.

HARGREAVES. I'm very sorry to hear that. That's very sad
    news.

JESS. Poppy killed herself because of your cuts. Is that all you
    can say?

HARGREAVES. You have my deepest...

KYLE. Oi! I may be in this chair but you are morally disabled!

HARGREAVES. Er... I would need to know more details
    before I can comment on a specific case. But I can see this is
    a very distressing topic for you all.

HENRY. Don't fucking patronise us!

BOB. Yeah, just answer the question!

MARCELLA. Yeah!   RITA. Exactly!

ANITA. We don't tolerate abusive language here.

BOB. Just abusive policies!

HARGREAVES. Look, please, make an appointment if there's
    something you wish to discuss with me.

ANITA *shows him a notification on her phone.*

Okay. I should inform you that the police are on their way.
You should all leave.

HARGREAVES *turns to leave.*

BOB. You walking away from us?

HARGREAVES. My staff must leave now. They must have the
freedom to leave. Please respect that.

HENRY. You lot love your talk of freedom, don't ya? Free
press, free markets. What are you free to do if you've no
money? Can you get on a train without a ticket? Can you
walk into a shop and help yourself? Try doing anything with
no money and you'll find out just how free you are!

HARGREAVES. Well, Henry, you are free to come and share
your concerns any time you wish.

HENRY. Shall I share my concerns then, Oliver? I'm now
homeless. My wife finally kicked me out because you lot
closed down the psychiatric centre that was treating me, and
I've become – and I'll try to be civil here – a friggin' basket
case. So now I wake up screaming under a bridge instead.
Oh, and my leg's got infected so now I'm on this fella.
(*Lifts up a crutch.*)

HARGREAVES. I'm sure we can discuss ways to help if you
make an appointment to see me.

MARCELLA. Is that all you can say to the poor man?

BOB. 'Make an appointment'? That's your answer to
everything!

The group cheers.

HARGREAVES. Please, everyone, whatever our differences,
remember, we are working hard to ensure previous mistakes
aren't repeated. I am listening. I am. And I truly believe we
can create a better functioning welfare system that ensures
those who genuinely need help receive it.

JESS. Do you know how hard it is to ask for help?

HARGREAVES. I really must ask you to leave now.

AIDAN. Dad, listen.

Beat.

JESS. Do you know how hard it is to ask for help? Your
government is making people like me beg for our basic
rights. You come into our homes and make us list what we
can't do. It's humiliating... You patronise us like we're
work-shy teenagers. Being wobbly isn't my problem. It's
living in a world that demonises difference.

The protesters cheer and clap. HARGREAVES *and* ANITA
hover nervously as the CAMERAPERSON *films* JESS.

But no one would choose to get a hundred pounds a week if
it meant they couldn't go toilet on their own, or make a cup
of tea, or leave their house. So this extra money that you're
making us beg for, it's not for nothing. It's because all those
things *you* do every day, without a second thought –
showering, buttering your toast, just walking – some of us
can't. I'd give your money back in a heartbeat if it meant I
could do those things. But I can't. No matter how much you
come and test me. And I'm not going to feel guilty any more.
Because we all have things we can't do and we all need help
sometimes. Even you. It's what makes us human.

They cheer, clap and stamp their feet.

HARGREAVES. I'd like to offer individual appointments with
anyone who wishes to discuss things further. But I suggest
you all move on before the police get here. / My staff do
need to leave now.

MARCELLA. Have they got an appointment?

ANITA. It's five-thirty. I need to pick up my boy.

The protesters start to unroll sleeping bags.

JESS. I can't leave my home when I want to.

RITA. I struggle to leave mine!

HENRY. I haven't got a home to leave!

KYLE. I'm trapped inside my home!

BOB. It's not a nice feeling being trapped, is it, folks?

ANITA. Why have you got sleeping bags?

MARCELLA. Because Poppy was stuck in bed without help.

HARGREAVES. Aidan, I strongly suggest you leave now.

AIDAN. I'm not going anywhere.

HARGREAVES. Aidan, come on!

KYLE (*to the camera now filming him*). They say disabled
     people don't have sex but millions of us are being fucked by
     his government every day!

BOB. You and your staff should 'just be patient'!

     HARGREAVES *turns to go and* HENRY *flings an adult
     nappy at him.*

HENRY. From Poppy!

HARGREAVES (*snapping*). This is ridiculous, childish
     behaviour! (*To* CAMERAPERSON.) Stop filming!

RITA. Just be patient, Mr Hargreaves!

HARGREAVES. I'm going to my office. Don't say you weren't
     warned. Anita!

     HARGREAVES *walks back into his office with* ANITA *and
     the* SOUND-WOMAN. *They try to get the*
     CAMERAPERSON *to follow but they stay and film.*

     *The protesters start to chant 'JUST BE PATIENT!', and bed
     down in their sleeping bags.*

     Moments later, OFFICER CHALFONT *arrives with several
     police officers, including a* FEMALE POLICE OFFICER
     and a MALE OFFICER. *The police tower over the group.*

OFFICER CHALFONT. Quieten down, please!

The protesters stop chanting.

Why are you here?

BOB. People in our community are dying. We just want answers.

The group agrees and claps.

OFFICER CHALFONT. Okay. Okay. Now, we've seen some of you before, haven't we? I remember making it clear that these protests wouldn't lead anywhere constructive. And yet here you are again.

HENRY. Where do you think the human rights you enjoy came from?!

OFFICER CHALFONT. Okay, Bono, calm down.

BOB. We're not going to stop protesting!

MARCELLA. Bob...!

OFFICER CHALFONT. Come on. These sorts of actions need to stop. You've made your point.

KYLE. What is our point?

JESS. Yeah!

OFFICER CHALFONT. I told you last time to keep your head down, lad.

HENRY. I fought in Iraq. Now I'm homeless. Do you think that's right?

OFFICER CHALFONT. We've had this conversation before if I'm not mistaken, sir.

HENRY. As a fellow human being, do you think it's right? I went to war for this country and now I'm sleeping under a fucking bridge!

OFFICER CHALFONT. Calm down. Now, this is private property. You all need to leave. If not, we will remove you. You have all been warned. Some of you multiple times.

Nobody moves.

I'm giving you one more warning. You can all leave now.
And we can all go home and have a nice, quiet evening.

Silence.

KYLE *starts to bang his wheelchair and chants 'JUST BE
PATIENT'.* HENRY *bangs his crutch on the floor and joins
in the chant, forcefully. They all start to chant. It is louder
this time.*

OFFICER CHALFONT *signals to his officers. They stop the*
CAMERAPERSON *filming.*

The police try to move KYLE*'s wheelchair but it won't
budge.* OFFICER CHALFONT *starts to pull the sleeping
bag off* KYLE. HENRY *yanks it out of* OFFICER
CHALFONT*'s hands. The crowd jeers.*

OFFICER CHALFONT *signals to his officers. One of them
shoves* HENRY *to the floor.*

An OFFICER *grabs* KYLE*'s jumper and, along with another*
OFFICER*, yanks him out of his wheelchair and onto the
floor.* AIDAN *and* HENRY *run to protect* KYLE *as he is
dragged away.* AIDAN *is intercepted by an* OFFICER *and
taken to one side;* HENRY *is shoved away. An* OFFICER
heads to MARCELLA*'s wheelchair.*

BOB *fights an* OFFICER *to stop* MARCELLA *being pushed
away.*

MARCELLA. That's my husband!

The OFFICER *starts to wheel* MARCELLA *away.* HENRY
*dumps his crutch, runs to the wheelchair and pushes it away
from the exit.* BOB *runs to the chair and helps* HENRY *to
stop it being wheeled out.* BOB *tries to shove the* OFFICER
away from the wheelchair. HENRY *shoves another*
OFFICER *away.* AIDAN *runs to the chair.*

BOB. Get the fuck off her!

MARCELLA *is tipped backwards out of her wheelchair and
dragged off.* HENRY*, shocked, is shoved away by an*

OFFICER. AIDAN *is knocked to the floor.* BOB *is wrestled away by officers and is led away, shouting.*

OFFICER CHALFONT. Clear the corner!

A FEMALE OFFICER *grabs* RITA. RITA *starts to scream.*

RITA. Don't touch me! Don't touch me! Please! Don't touch me! Don't touch me! Please!

JESS *grabs the* FEMALE OFFICER*'s leg and tries to get her to release* RITA.

JESS. Please don't touch her! She doesn't like being touched!

RITA *continues to scream. She backs off, hysterical, out the exit, followed by an* OFFICER.

JESS *is pulled away from the* FEMALE OFFICER *by a* MALE OFFICER.

AIDAN *runs over to protect* JESS *but he's knocked over by an* OFFICER.

HENRY (*to the* OFFICER *who knocked over* AIDAN). Oh, you're the big man!

The officers step closer.

HENRY *brandishes his crutch as a weapon.*

Pigs in uniform! (*Swinging his crutch at them.*) I used to be like you!

The OFFICERS *grapple with* HENRY *and handcuff him.*

(*To* OFFICER CHALFONT.) You know, what happened to me can happen to anyone. You, your kid. Anyone can become sick or disabled at any time! Can you imagine that?

The police drag HENRY *away.*

Can you imagine anything? Didn't think so…

JESS *and* AIDAN *kneel down and link arms.* OFFICER CHALFONT *towers over them.*

OFFICER CHALFONT. I hope you're seeing how pointless this all is.

HARGREAVES *has come out of his office to see what is happening.*

AIDAN. You going to let them arrest us all, Dad? For this? Seriously?

OFFICER CHALFONT. What do you want us to do, sir?

HARGREAVES *looks at* OFFICER CHALFONT, *then at* AIDAN, *then at* JESS.

Sir?

An OFFICER *enters.*

OFFICER. Sir, we need you. There's a situation outside.

OFFICER CHALFONT. I'll be back. Don't move.

He runs out.

AIDAN. Well?

HARGREAVES. Grow up, Aidan. If you break the rules, there are consequences.

AIDAN. What if you break people?

AIDAN *reaches into his bag. He pulls out the painting that* HARGREAVES *painted as a boy. He unfolds it. The two parts have been stuck together.*

AIDAN *holds it up to* HARGREAVES.

I put him back together.

HARGREAVES *can't believe his eyes. He walks over to* AIDAN *and takes the painting.*

JESS *stands up. We hear shouting outside.*

HARGREAVES, *still holding the painting and staring at it, walks away slowly.*

It's beautiful.

HARGREAVES *stops.*

You were beautiful, Dad.

HARGREAVES *turns to look at* AIDAN. *They stare at each other across the office.*

I wish I'd known that boy.

JESS. Oli.

HARGREAVES *turns to* JESS.

We can do better. Can't you see what this system is doing… To all of us?

HARGREAVES *stares at* JESS.

The End.

www.nickhernbooks.co.uk

facebook.com/nickhernbooks

twitter.com/nickhernbooks